INSPIRING SPORTS STORIES

FOR KIDS

BEN BYDE

TABLE OF CONTENTS

INTRODUCTION

Welcome to the captivating world of sports, where resilience meets passion, and dreams touch the sky! You're about to embark on an exhilarating journey through the lives of some of the most iconic sports figures to ever live.

In this book, we'll venture into the lives of fifteen extraordinary athletes from all walks of life. Each of these sports heroes started their journey just like you, as kids with big dreams. They faced challenges, stumbled, got up, and pushed forward, turning their dreams into realities. Their stories aren't merely about winning games or breaking records. They are tales of the human spirit, tenacity, perseverance, and the power of believing in oneself.

From the football fields of Portugal where Cristiano Ronaldo honed his skills, to the powerful waves of Hawaii that tested the courage of Bethany Hamilton; from the competitive world of Formula One where Lewis Hamilton broke barriers, to the boxing ring where Muhammad Ali danced like a butterfly and stung like a bee—this collection of stories will take you on a journey around the world and into the lives of these exceptional individuals.

Each of these stories, woven with facts and sprinkled with details, will engage, entertain, and most of all inspire you. You will laugh, you may cry, but you will definitely learn.

You'll learn about resilience, hard work, overcoming adversity, and standing up for what you believe in. You'll understand that winning isn't just about crossing the finish line first, but about the journey, the struggles, and the triumph of the human spirit.

So buckle up, young readers, and get ready for a thrilling ride through the highs and lows, the trials and triumphs, of some of the greatest athletes the world has ever seen.

Let's step into their shoes, run their races, and discover what it truly takes to be a champion.

After all, every champion was once a child who dared to dream.

Now, it's your turn.

CRISTIANO RONALDO
"CR7"

Moscow, 2008. UEFA Champions League final. Manchester United's star, Cristiano Ronaldo, against Chelsea's goal keeper, Edwin van der Sar. The roar of 70,000 fans was a cauldron of sound, "Ronaldo! Ronaldo!" echoing off the rafters.

Cristiano Ronaldo stood on the dew-kissed turf, his heart pounding like a drum. It was the UEFA Champions League final, tied in extra time, the ball at his feet. It all came down to this penalty shootout.

Cristiano, in his bright red jersey, stood 12 yards from his destiny. His pulse raced, matching the pounding heartbeat of the crowd. Memories of his small island home, Madeira, and the worn-out football of his childhood filled his mind.

This was a defining moment, but it was one chapter in the extraordinary journey of a boy from Madeira becoming a football legend.

Inhale. Run. Kick...

Before we tell you how this match ends, let's turn back the pages. Back to Madeira, where it all began for a young boy with dreams bigger than his island home.

In the heart of the Atlantic Ocean, far from the bustling cities and famous football stadiums of mainland Europe, lies the small island of Madeira, Portugal. This was where our hero's journey began.

Cristiano Ronaldo dos Santos Aveiro was born on February 5th, 1985, in the small town of Funchal, into a humble family. His father, José Dinis Aveiro, worked as a gardener and his mother, Maria Dolores dos Santos, was a cook. They lived in a small tin-roofed home that overlooked the ocean, a constant reminder of their seclusion from the rest of the world.

From an early age, Cristiano had a restless energy about him. He was constantly on the move, seeking an outlet for his vibrant spirit. That outlet came in the form of an old, half broken, worn-out soccer ball.

Cristiano would spend hours kicking it around the dusty streets of Madeira, losing himself in the thrill and freedom of the game. The world beyond his island might have been out of reach, but in these moments, with a ball at his feet, Cristiano felt limitless.

Cristiano's father, who was also the part time equipment manager at the local boys' soccer club, would often bring home discarded football gear for his son to use.

One of Cristiano's earliest mentors was his youth coach at Andorinha, the local club his father worked for. He saw how Cristiano loved the game and how hard he worked.

Recognizing his talent, the coach nurtured his abilities and taught him a crucial lesson that Cristiano would carry with him throughout his career: "Hard work is just as important as talent, Cristiano."

Cristiano would arrive at the club as soon as the sun peeked over the mountains and would only leave when the stars came out. He loved the game, and it showed. Each practice he attended, each game, he shone brighter, his skills dazzled, and boy, was he fast!

José, his Dad, was always there, cheering him on from the side lines. Times were hard and they didn't have much, but José made sure Cristiano never missed a match.

By the age of 10, everyone on the island knew Cristiano Ronaldo, the football wonder.

Cristiano took a giant leap at just 12 years old. It was 1997, and he left his beloved island of Madeira for the bustling city of Lisbon to join Sporting CP, one of Portugal's top football clubs. This was like moving from a cosy pond to an enormous ocean. He was homesick and missed the warmth of his family and the familiarity of his home island. . The city kids would tease him for his foreign Madeiran accent, but Cristiano just let his football do the talking. The spirit of the island boy who dreamt of playing under the big stadium lights was undeterred.

At 15, Cristiano faced a hurdle that seemed taller than the highest mountain. During a routine check-up, doctors discovered something troubling - his heart was beating way too fast, even when he wasn't running or playing. They called it a 'racing heart.' It was a condition that could have put a full stop to his football dreams.

This was scary. Imagine, you're 15 and you're told that your heart, the very thing that keeps you alive, might stop you from doing what you love most. The bullies who mocked him and the pains of being poor seemed small in comparison to this challenge. But remember what we learned from Cristiano? No setback was too big for him.

With a brave heart (and a racing one at that), Cristiano decided to face this challenge head-on. His mom, Maria, convinced him to go for the operation that would help fix his heart. The procedure was a success, and after a short recovery, Cristiano was back on the football field, his heart beating with joy this time, and no longer racing with fear.

In August 2003, during a friendly match against Manchester United, 18-year-old Cristiano's performance was so dazzling that it caught the eye of the manager, Sir Alex Ferguson. He saw the raw talent in Cristiano, and knew he could help shape him into a world-class player.

"He's the one," Ferguson declared after the match, "We need him in our squad." By the end of August 2003, Cristiano Ronaldo became a part of Manchester United, stepping into the big leagues and donning the iconic red jersey.

Life at Manchester United was a quantum leap from what Cristiano knew. The city's biting cold was a far cry from the sunny climate of Madeira and Lisbon. The competition was fierce, and the expectations? Sky-high. But in Sir Alex Ferguson, Cristiano found more than a coach. He found a mentor, a guide, and a steadfast supporter.

One such moment was during an early training session, where Cristiano's flair was present, but his lack of focus was also apparent.

"Cristiano," Ferguson had told him in his no-nonsense manner, " your talent is undeniable. But without hard work, talent means nothing. Remember, the best players are also the hardest workers." "

These words struck a chord with Cristiano, harking back to the advice given by his first coach. Under Ferguson's watchful eye, he honed his craft tirelessly, his work ethic matching his natural skill. He trained harder, played smarter, and became a critical asset to the team.

His transformation was evident. The flashy young winger evolved into a lethal forward. His speed, his powerful free kicks, and his uncanny ability to find the back of the net made him a fan favorite..

In September 2005, Cristiano faced the toughest challenge of them all. But this time it wasn't on the football field. He was only 20 and playing for Manchester United, away in Russia. In the early hours of the morning he received a call that shattered his world. He received the heart breaking news that his beloved dad, José, had passed away of liver failure. This was a huge loss for Cristiano, and he was completely devastated. His father, who had cheered him on from the sidelines since his earliest days in football, was no longer there.

Despite his deep sadness, Cristiano showed his courage. The very next day, he decided to play in the match representing his country, Portugal, against Russia. When asked why he still played in that match, Cristiano said, "My dad, my biggest fan, would have wanted me to play. This match is for him."

Cristiano played his heart out that day. Every sprint, every pass, every shot at the goal was a tribute to his dad. And though his dad wasn't there to cheer him from the sidelines, Cristiano knew he was watching from above, very proud of his son.

In the midst of the 2006 football season, the Manchester United squad was prepping for a critical match against Arsenal. Cristiano Ronaldo, already an emerging star, had been dazzling on the field but the team had been on a 4 game losing streak. Sir Alex Ferguson, known for his wisdom and knack for nurturing talent, sensed the need for a heart-to-heart.

"Cristiano," Ferguson said one afternoon during training, his voice a mix of sternness and care, "you're a fantastic player, truly top-class."

Cristiano listened, always eager to absorb Ferguson's advice.

"But remember," Ferguson continued, his gaze serious, "it's the team that makes you shine. Football is a team sport. Your personal brilliance will be remembered more if the team succeeds."

That chat was a game changer for Ronaldo. It shifted his focus towards teamwork, which in turn, led to Manchester United clinching multiple victories in the following seasons.

By 2007, with the help of his team, he was the top scorer in the Premier League.

And in 2008, with Cristiano at the helm, Manchester United won the UEFA Champions League, the pinnacle of club football.

The penalty kick that opened this story found the back of the net and made Manchester United the best team in all of Europe.

Later that year, in the cold winter of Paris, a murmur of anticipation filled the air. Dressed in a sharp tuxedo, Cristiano Ronaldo watched as the envelope was unsealed at a prestigious FIFA event. He had been here before, but this time, the stakes were much higher. The name called out was his, and Cristiano Ronaldo, the island boy from Madeira, had won his first Ballon d'Or, an honor of the highest order, recognizing him as the best footballer in the world.

Tears filled his eyes as he recalled the people who had made this moment possible - his family, his friends, his mentor Sir Alex, his teammates, and of course his father. He felt an overwhelming sense of pride and satisfaction but knew this was only the beginning.

Ronaldo embarked on the next phase of his extraordinary journey - a prestigious move to Real Madrid.

There, beneath the vibrant Spanish sun, he graced the fields of the Santiago Bernabeu Stadium.

His amazing skills, along with teamwork from the whole squad, led Real Madrid to many big wins. They won two Spanish League titles, two Copa del Rey trophies, and an incredible four Champions League titles! This showed everyone that Real Madrid was the best in Europe.

In a post match interview after Ronaldo scored a hattrick against fierce rivals, Atletico Madrid he replied,

"Scoring goals is a great feeling, but the most important thing to me is that the team is successful – it doesn't matter who scores the goals as long as we're winning."

Ronaldo was making a name for himself at Real Madrid, becoming one of the greatest footballers ever. But he was not done yet.

In 2018, Ronaldo took on a new challenge. He moved to Juventus, a club in Italy also known as the 'Old Lady' and donned the iconic black and white stripes. Moving from Madrid to Italy was like jumping into a whole new world. But, just as before, he adjusted to his new surroundings quickly. Ronaldo had a big goal: he wanted to win in Italy, just like he had in England and Spain.

Ronaldo, the boy from a small island in Portugal, had now made a mark in England with Manchester United, in Spain with Real Madrid, and in Italy with Juventus. In each of these nations, Ronaldo had risen to the top, guided his team to victory, and etched his name into footballing history.

Then, in the summer of 2021, the football world held its breath as whispers of a remarkable homecoming began to swirl. Cristiano Ronaldo, the prodigal son of Manchester United, was on the verge of a sensational return. The same boy who had left Old Trafford as a promising talent more than a decade ago, was now returning as one of the greatest footballers of all time.

When Ronaldo first set foot on the lush green turf of Old Trafford in 2003, he was an 18-year-old lad from Madeira, brimming with potential. Now, he was returning as a seasoned veteran, a decorated superstar, a leader with immense experience and unquenchable hunger for success.

His first match back on the old turf against the Magpies, Newcastle United, did not disappoint.

With the floodlights casting long, dancing shadows on the lush green pitch, Ronaldo emerged from the tunnel dressed in the legendary number 7 shirt..

In the last minutes, the crowd held its breath as Ronaldo found himself faced with two opposing defenders. They were like two giants, ready to pounce on the ball at Ronaldo's feet. But Ronaldo wasn't one to back down. A determined glint in his eyes, he expertly flicked the ball over the first defender's outstretched leg.

The crowd gasped, their eyes glued to the spectacle unfolding on the pitch. Ronaldo was quick, a blur of red and white – that how fast he moved. a The second defender, startled by Ronaldo's speed, fumbled in his attempt to intercept, and was quickly left in his dust.

Now, he was faced with the goalkeeper, the last line of defense. Ronaldo glanced over his shoulder, spotting his teammate, Luke Shaw, open on his right. In a lightning-fast move, he sent the ball spinning towards him. "Show them, Cristiano!" Shaw quipped, as he swiftly returned the ball to Ronaldo.

With a speed and precision honed over the years, Ronaldo didn't miss a beat. He met the ball with his boot mid-air at the perfect angle, sending it rocketing over the goalkeeper's outstretched arms and into the back of the net.

The cheers from the crowd echoed around the stadium, a roar of jubilation that marked the return of their hero. The kid from Madeira had done it again, and this time, he was home.

As we look at Ronaldo today, he is still out there, doing what he loves.. Despite the whispers of retirement, Ronaldo is relentless, his love for the game undimmed. He's still out there on the training grounds, first to arrive, last to leave, setting the bar high for those around him and for future generations.

The legacy of Cristiano Ronaldo is much more than the sum of his awards and records. It's about his resilience, his unwavering self-belief, his insatiable hunger for success, and his commitment to hard work. These are the lessons he learned on his journey, lessons he shares with every young dreamer who dares to aim high.

MICHAEL PHELPS: "THE FLYING FISH"

It's the night of August 9, 2016 - the finals of the 200m butterfly at the Olympic Games in Rio de Janeiro. Michael Phelps, standing at an impressive 6'4", is at the poolside, his eyes set on the glistening water that awaits him. He knows that this is the ultimate test of his career, the moment that would define his legacy.

He's not just swimming against other Olympians; he's swimming against his past and against the current world record of 1:51.51, a mark he himself set eight years earlier in Beijing. Phelps isn't just gunning for gold; he's aiming to break the barrier once again, pushing the limits of human speed in water. The stakes couldn't be higher, and the world is watching, collectively holding its breath.

His competitors, some of the fastest swimmers in the world, are eyeing the same prize. There's Chad le Clos, the South African swimmer who'd edged out Phelps to take gold in this event at the London Olympics four years earlier. There's also Laszlo Cseh from Hungary, another seasoned butterfly specialist, whose time in the preliminaries was faster than Phelps'. But no matter who he's up against, Phelps knows that the biggest challenge is always within.

As the buzzer sounds, they dive in. The crowd roars as they watch Phelps transform into the 'Flying Fish.' This is the moment we've all been waiting for, the grand finale in the epic journey of Michael Phelps.

But before we get swept up in the thrill of this race, let's rewind the clock and find out how this water-loving boy from Baltimore became the greatest swimmer the world has ever seen.

Back in 1985 in the lively city of Baltimore, long before all of the medals and records, a baby boy named Michael Phelps entered the world. From a very young age, Michael was a water baby, and he could hardly stay out of it!

His mother, Debbie, would often share the story of how she couldn't keep Michael away from water. She'd laugh and recall, "Even bath time turned into an epic water splash! Michael would kick and wriggle like a little fish." It was no surprise when she decided to take her water-loving baby for swimming lessons.

As Michael grew, so did his love for swimming. He enjoyed the feeling of moving freely in the water, of being weightless, and the soothing rhythm of his own breath. To him, swimming was more than just a hobby. It was a passion that flowed through his veins.

Michael, a kid with ADHD, found school hard. The loud school bell and the coming lessons would make him scared. The classroom was like a war zone filled with hard words and numbers.

Staying still and focusing felt like trying to climb the highest mountain.

One hot summer day, Michael went to the pool to cool down. The sun was shining bright, and the town was quiet except for the sound of the leaves moving in the wind. Michael, who was just eight, jumped into the pool.

The cool water made him feel peaceful. He realized swimming was not just a way to escape the heat, it was magical. It was like the water was singing a calming song that only he could hear.

In the classroom, Michael couldn't focus. His mind would jump from one thought to another like a butterfly in a garden. But in the pool, it was different. He could swim for hours. The steady beat of his heart and the quiet sound of the pool helped him focus. The pool was his safe place.

Swimming helped Michael use his energy in a good way. The excitement of racing, the rush of winning, and the discipline it required helped him manage his ADHD. The pool was where he found what he loved to do.

Every time Michael swam, he was doing more than just exercise. He was learning to take his ADHD, which made him feel jumpy and distracted, and use it to push himself harder

In Michael's own words, "Swimming is normal for me. I'm relaxed. I'm comfortable, and I know my surroundings. It's my home." This is where he channelled his ADHD, turning a challenge into an advantage.

Phelps, a young boy with big dreams, found his guiding light at the North Baltimore Aquatic Club. His life changed when he met Bob Bowman, a man who would become more than just a coach to him.

Bob Bowman was a man known for his stern discipline and unique training techniques. When he first met Michael, he saw potential in the energetic and determined boy. But he knew potential wasn't enough; it needed discipline and hard work to bloom.

Michael's training routine was anything but ordinary. His day began when the stars were still shining bright in the early morning sky. Yawning and rubbing sleep out of his eyes, he would prepare for the long journey to the pool. Despite the chill of the dawn and the distance from home, he never faltered.

At the pool, under the steady gaze of Coach Bob, the real grind would begin. The cold water would be an initial shock, but he didn't flinch, immersing himself in the grueling routine. Hours would slip by as he swam lap after lap, his body screaming for rest, but he pushed on

One cold evening, when he was particularly exhausted, Bob gave him a piece of advice that stuck.

He said, "Michael, remember, this pool isn't just about learning to swim, it's about learning to be resilient, to face your ADHD head on and use it to your advantage."

Those words hit home. Michael realized that the pool was more than just a swimming arena, it was a battleground where he was not just battling his physical limits, but also his ADHD. Every early morning, every long drive, every freezing dive into the pool, and every late-night lap, were all part of his greater journey to conquer his ADHD and become the best swimmer he could be.

In 2000, Michael Phelps, barely 15, became the youngest American male swimmer at an Olympic Games in nearly 70 years. This was a monumental stride. The Olympics were far from just another swim meet - they represented the apex of global athletic competition.

When Michael arrived in Sydney, a whirlwind of emotions surged within him. Excitement and anxiety intertwined as he stood amidst the world's finest athletes, the immense crowd, and the symbolic Olympic rings omnipresent. It felt surreal, like a dream, but Michael knew it was his reality. It was his first shot at demonstrating his potential to the world.

In the pool, Michael swam with all his might. But his opponents, mostly in their early to mid-twenties, and with more experience under their belts, matched him stroke for stroke. Despite his relentless efforts, Michael fell short. He ended up finishing fifth in the 200m butterfly, his only event in these Games.

Michael took it as a pivotal learning opportunity. He observed his competitors, their techniques, their discipline, their tenacity. The realization hit him that success at this level required more than just raw energy and passion. It requires relentless hard work, building physical and mental strength, and an indomitable spirit.

"In Sydney, I learned that the Olympics is not just about winning medals," Michael would reflect. "It's about giving your best, learning, and growing. It's about fighting till the end, no matter what."

Michael returned from Sydney without a medal, but what he brought back was far more precious - invaluable experience and lessons that would steer his future trajectory, making him the legend he was destined to become.

Four years after Sydney, Michael Phelps was ready for the 2004 Athens Olympics. He was older, stronger, and more skilled. He wanted to win gold.

When he got to Athens, Michael was excited and focused. The big stadium, the loud crowd, and the sight of the pool made him want to win even more. He was ready to do his best and make history.

In the pool, Michael was strong and fast. Every stroke and turn he made was perfect. He swam very well, breaking records and winning his first gold medals.

His first gold medal came in the 400m individual medley. He beat his own world record and finished way ahead of the other swimmers. This was a huge moment for Michael, but he didn't stop there.

Michael won six gold medals in total, including two in relay races. He also won two bronze medals. One of his best races was the 200m butterfly, where he swam much faster than the other swimmers.

Winning gold was a dream come true for Michael. But it wasn't just about the medals. It was about the hard work, the lessons learned, and the journey to get there. It was about becoming the best swimmer in the world.

In 2008, Michael went on to win a record-breaking 8 gold medals at the Beijing Olympics. However, after the high of this victory, a low followed. After the London Olympics in 2012, where he won four gold and two silver medals, Michael decided to retire. He felt burnt out and uncertain of his future.

With support from his loved ones, Michael found his strength again. He understood that life, like the waves, has its ups and downs, and he was ready to navigate through it all.

In 2014, after two years of retirement, Michael Phelps made a startling announcement: he was returning to professional swimming. This decision took everyone by surprise, but Michael had rekindled his love for the sport.

Returning to swimming wasn't a walk in the park. His body had aged; it was no longer the young, flexible body he was used to. Despite the challenges, a renewed passion for the sport kept him motivated.

By 2016, after two grueling years of training, Michael was ready to make a splash at the Rio Olympics. There was excitement, nerves, but also a sense of peace. He was doing what he loved – that was the true victory for him.

In Rio, Phelps competed in six races. He left no room for doubts or hesitation in the pool. He won five gold medals: in 200m butterfly, 200m individual medley, 4x100m freestyle relay, 4x200m freestyle relay, and 4x100m medley relay. He also took silver in the 100m butterfly.

One of the memorable races was the 200m butterfly. Michael finished with a time of 1:53.36, beating out Japan's Masato Sakai by just four hundredths of a second. This victory was a full circle moment for Michael, as this was the same event in which he had finished 5th as a 15-year-old at the Sydney Olympics in 2000.

In the end, Michael's comeback was triumphant. He finished his career with a staggering total of 28 medals, 23 of them gold, solidifying his legacy as the most decorated Olympian of all time.

Michael, the most decorated Olympian of all time, was not always the revered figure he is today. His journey to the pinnacle of swimming was fraught with adversity, both in and out of the pool.

As a child, Phelps was often the target of bullies. His large ears, the fact that he shaved his legs, and his choice to wear a speedo were all points of mockery. The bullying was relentless and deeply upsetting, but Phelps eventually reached a point where he simply stopped caring about the taunts. He had bigger goals to achieve, and he wouldn't let the opinions of others deter him. His mother, Debbie Phelps, recalls how her son even wore a baseball hat to hide his ears, but the bullying persisted. She advised him to be the stronger person and walk away, a lesson that Phelps took to heart.

Phelps' physical attributes, while a source of mockery in his childhood, turned out to be his greatest advantages in the pool. His large feet acted like flippers, propelling him through the water with unmatched speed. His long arms gave him a reach that few could compete with. But perhaps his most significant advantage was his ability to stay underwater longer than most other swimmers after kicking off from the wall. This skill, combined with his physical attributes, made him a formidable force in the pool.

One of the most iconic moments in Phelps' career came during the 400-meter freestyle relay at the Rio Olympics. The American team was considered an underdog, and Phelps, at 31, was seen as past his prime. Yet, when Phelps was the second man in the water for the American relay team, he produced what his coach, Bob Bowman, called "probably the best turn that's ever been done underwater." This turn, a series of furious dolphin kicks off the wall, essentially ended the race, even with 250 meters to go. Phelps emerged with a commanding lead that only grew as he churned for home. The American team won gold, marking their first 400 free relay gold since the 2009 World Championships.

Phelps' journey is a testament to resilience and determination. His story is a reminder that adversity can be overcome, that the attributes that make us different can be our greatest strengths, and that with hard work and dedication, we can turn our trials into triumphs.

The year was 2017. Serena was playing on a bright, sunlit court at the Australian Open, ready to serve for the match. She was on the verge of winning her 23rd Grand Slam title, a victory that would seal her place in tennis history. Serena's heart pounded in her chest like a drum, echoing the roaring applause of the crowd.

The tension in the air was so thick you could almost cut it with a knife. The crowd held its collective breath as Serena prepared to serve, their eager eyes reflecting the clear blue Australian sky. With each bounce of the ball against the court, Serena reminded herself of the words she once said: "The only pressure I feel is the pressure I put on myself to win."

On the other side of the net stood not just any opponent, but her own flesh and blood, Venus Williams, her sister. Venus, both a rival and a constant source of inspiration, faced her with a determined look of concentration. This added a whole new dimension to Serena's quest - it was about victory and balancing the delicate equilibrium of family ties. As Serena tossed the ball into the air, time seemed to slow down. She struck the ball with her racket, and it whizzed across the net like a comet shooting across the sky.

The crowd watched as the ball ricocheted off her opponent's racket and sailed out of bounds. Serena's heart leaped with joy. She had done it. She had surpassed Steffi Graf, winning her 23rd Grand Slam, a feat unparalleled in the modern era of tennis. The crowd erupted in thunderous applause.

But this was just the climax of Serena's remarkable journey. To truly appreciate this moment, we must travel back to where it all began.

In 1981, a star was born in the bustling city of Compton, California. Her name was Serena Williams. Compton was a tough place with high crime rates, economic hardship, and limited opportunities. It was a place where the harsh realities of poverty often overshadowed dreams. Yet, for Serena, it was home.

Serena and her sister, Venus, were inseparable since birth, bound by their shared love for a game played with a fuzzy yellow ball and a racket. Their father, Richard Williams, introduced them to tennis, a sport that would later bring them worldwide fame. "I decided to teach my daughters tennis," he once said, "because I saw it as a path to a better life for them."

Richard would often take the girls to a local park, where they would hit tennis balls against a concrete wall. The strike of the tennis ball against the hard surface was a common soundtrack to Serena's childhood. Serena found her sanctuary on the court with her sister by her side and a racket in her hand.

The family's humble court was a stark contrast to the plush green lawns of Wimbledon, but to Serena, it was paradise. It was here that Serena learned to hit her first backhand, served her first ace, and learned an essential life lesson—to keep her eyes on the ball, both literally and metaphorically.

Serena and Venus were more than just sisters, they were each other's best friends. Together, they embarked on a journey through the world of junior tennis. In every win and every loss, they were there for each other. This special bond they shared became their most potent strength.

Their early days on the tennis circuit were not a cakewalk. Every morning with physically demanding practice sessions, tough matches that tested their limits, and relentless travel, the sisters lived a life beyond their tender ages.

One such morning was particularly unforgettable. The girls were preparing for a challenging match in the junior circuit against the top-seeded duo in the junior doubles championship. As Serena, the younger of the two and slightly less experienced, practiced her serves, anxiety was evident on her face. But their father and coach, Richard, was their pillar of strength. He encouraged them, pushed them to their limits, and never let them forget their potential.

"Remember," Richard said, noticing Serena's anxiety, "you're a champion in the making. You've got Venus by your side, and there's nothing you two can't achieve together."

"I was so lucky to have a sister like Venus. She was always there for me," Serena would often say about those early days. Venus, older and more experienced, was Serena's guiding star through the tricky maze of competitive tennis.

The match day arrived, and with it came the rush of adrenaline. The sisters found themselves a set down, and their opponents were formidable. But Serena and Venus, they were fighters. They rallied, encouraged each other, and, most importantly, never lost hope. After a grueling tiebreaker, the sisters emerged victorious. This victory brought them closer together, strengthening their bond like never before.

The world of professional tennis was vast and intimidating for the young girls from Compton. But they had each other, and that was all they needed. The victories tasted sweeter when celebrated together, and the losses were less harsh when they had each other for support. "Venus and I have shared everything together. She is my rock, and I am hers," Serena would often say.

Together, they were not just Venus and Serena; they were the mighty Williams Sisters, ready to conquer the world.

Richard Williams was not just Serena's father; he was her first coach, her guiding light, and her biggest supporter. From the raw streets of Compton to the grand stadiums of international tennis, he was always by her side, instilling in her the lessons that would shape her life and career.

One day, after a particularly challenging practice session, a young Serena found herself upset over not getting her serves right. Seeing her frustration, Richard sat down beside her and said, "Remember, baby girl, the world of tennis is a lot like life. It's not just about how you serve or how hard you can hit the ball. It's about how you respond when things don't go your way."

However, as Serena's passion for tennis grew, so did her hunger for more ambitious challenges. She was ready to take her game to the next level; for that, she needed a new environment that could match her aspirations.

And so, the Williams family made a monumental decision—they packed their bags and moved across the country to sunny Florida, a move that would prove pivotal in Serena's journey. Florida was home to some of the best tennis training academies in the country, and it was here that Serena and Venus would meet their new coach, Rick Macci.

Rick was known for his no-nonsense approach to coaching and his ability to bring out the best in his players. He saw the spark in Serena and Venus and knew he could fan it into a flame. "I'm not here to teach you tennis; I'm here to make you champions," he would often say.

Under Rick's tutelage, Serena's game evolved. She honed her signature serve, a powerful weapon that would win her many matches in the future. She developed her footwork, her strategies, and her mental toughness. Rick taught Serena not just to play the game but to own it. "You have to believe in yourself when no one else does," Rick would say, words that resonated deeply with Serena.

With a new home, a new coach, and an unwavering spirit, Serena was well on her way to making her mark in the world of tennis.

Serena's dreams took flight when she stepped onto the professional courts at the age of fourteen. It may have been daunting for some to face seasoned opponents at such a young age, but Serena was different. She was ready to show the world what she was made of.

To many, the idea of challenging veteran competitors while still in their early teens may have been overwhelming, but Serena was different. The world of professional tennis, where the average age of players was around 24, was ready to meet this youthful prodigy.

Her first professional match took place in Quebec City, Canada, on an October day, in front of an audience of about a thousand spectators. The crowd, used to watching experienced, seasoned players, now saw a young girl take the court. The opponent she faced was a well-ranked player, skilled and seasoned in the game. Under the glare of the bright stadium lights and the amplified sound of the cheering crowd, Serena, in spite of her jittery nerves, held her ground.

Even though she didn't win that day, she learned a valuable lesson: "I've grown most not from victories, but setbacks," she later reflected.

Serena's first steps on the professional courts were not just about tennis; they were about growing up, learning to handle pressure, and staying true to oneself. With each match, Serena was not just playing tennis but shaping her path to greatness. And this was just the beginning.

In 1999, Serena, just seventeen years old, played in a significant tennis competition, the U.S. Open. Winning this competition is known as a "Grand Slam" victory, which is like winning a gold medal at the Olympics - a massive deal in tennis!

As she entered the tournament, Serena was an underdog, underestimated by many but unflinching in her self-belief. She had her eyes on the prize and was determined to give it her all. The matches were tough, and the opponents were challenging, but Serena stood firm.

When Serena found herself in the final, facing off against world-class player Martina Hingis, who had already tasted victory at numerous grand slam tournaments.

The day of the final, Arthur Ashe Stadium was packed. Tens of thousands of fans had gathered to watch the spectacle, the air buzzing with anticipation. Martina Hingis, then the number one player in the world, was favored to win. But Serena wasn't easily intimidated.

As Serena walked onto the court, she was greeted by the crowd's loud cheers. She looked across the net, seeing Martina Hingis on the other side. It was a thrilling moment - the young, aspiring player about to face the seasoned, world-class champion.

The match began, and right from the start, it was clear that Serena was not going to back down. Despite Hingis's attempts to dominate the game with her tactical prowess, Serena fought back with her powerful serve and aggressive groundstrokes.

As the match went on, Serena's confidence grew. She blasted her forehand shots past Hingis and kept her on the run. Her powerful serves were difficult for Hingis to return. In the rallies, Serena's speed and agility helped her return shots that looked out of reach.

By the time they reached the final set, the crowd was on the edge of their seats. Serena was just a few games away from winning. With her relentless determination and focus, Serena finally hit the winning shot - a powerful backhand Hingis couldn't return. The crowd erupted in cheers.

This win propelled Serena into the global spotlight, her name synonymous with talent, power, and perseverance. Fans, critics, and fellow players alike began to see Serena as a force to be reckoned with in the world of tennis.

But more than the fame and the accolades, this victory had a profound impact on Serena. It affirmed her self-belief and fueled her ambition. she once said. "That first Grand Slam win ... it was a taste of what I could achieve if I set my mind to it."

The year 2003 started as promising for Serena, but an unexpected injury threw a wrench into her plans. During one of her routine practices, she felt a sharp pain in her knee, a pain that would later be diagnosed as a severe knee injury. It was a crushing blow for Serena. Tennis was her life, and suddenly, she was benched.

She often recounts, "There I was at the top of my game, and suddenly, I was on the sidelines. But I knew I wasn't out. I couldn't let this be the end of my story." Serena's spirit refused to be quenched. She fought through the pain, the surgeries, and the grueling rehab.

In 2011, just when things started looking up, she was confronted with an even scarier health crisis. She was diagnosed with a pulmonary embolism, a deadly condition where a blood clot blocks an artery in the lungs. If you think of your lungs as a busy city with lots of cars (which are like blood cells), a pulmonary embolism is like a giant traffic jam that stops everything in its tracks.

Her recovery from this was quite lengthy. Serena spent nearly a year, from the summer of 2010 until the summer of 2011, dealing with her health issues, including the pulmonary embolism and subsequent treatment, before returning to competitive tennis.

She demonstrated that she was a champion on the tennis court and in the game of life.

In the world of sports, rivals can often push us to our limits, testing our abilities and compelling us to strive for better. For Serena, this rival came in the form of Maria Sharapova. From the moment Sharapova stepped onto the court as a teenager, it was clear a compelling rivalry was taking shape.

Their matches were a spectacle, a clash of titans, filled with high-powered serves and razor-sharp returns. Sharapova was among the few players who could match Serena's intensity on the court.

One of the most memorable moments in their rivalry was the 2004 Wimbledon final. Sharapova, just seventeen, managed to beat Serena, surprising everyone. The match was a close one. Both players gave their all, but in the end, Sharapova's solid serves and determined returns won her the match. Serena took the loss gracefully, saying, "It's not about how you fall; it's about how you get back up."

This rivalry was not about hatred but respect, competition, and the desire to improve. "Rivalry with Maria has made me a better player. It's pushed me to dig deep and discover new layers of my game," Serena said.

The Serena-Sharapova rivalry was more than just a series of matches. It was a testament to the spirit of competition, the thrill of the game, and the unyielding desire to be the best. Their battles on the court were legendary, an integral part of the grand narrative of women's tennis.

Back to the pivotal moment we first met Serena at the start of the story—the 2017 Australian Open Final. The stage was set for an epic showdown between two exceptional athletes and sisters, Serena and Venus Williams. This was more than just a tennis match; it was a clash of titans, a landmark in sporting history that will never be forgotten.

There was a buzz in the air in the run-up to the final match. Serena had already secured 22 Grand Slam titles, equalling the record of the legendary Steffi Graf. Now, she was on the brink of breaking that record. But to do so, she had to defeat her sister, Venus, an extraordinary tennis player in her own right.

It wasn't just the record that was on Serena's mind. This was also about family pride, the incredible journey the Williams sisters had made from the tough streets of Compton to the glamorous world of professional tennis. "It was like a flashback," Serena would later say, "from when we were little girls dreaming about this moment, and now it was happening."

The night before the match, as Serena lay in her hotel room, she remembered the many obstacles she had overcome to get here—the long hours of practice, the injuries, the setbacks, the triumphs, and the defeats. "All of it had led me to this moment," she recalled.

The morning of the match was a whirl of activity. As she warmed up on the court, Serena felt a mix of anticipation and excitement. She looked across the net at her sister, Venus, knowing they were about to make history together.

The match's first serve flew from Serena's racket, marking the start of a memorable battle. The match was a roller coaster, with both sisters giving their all, their powerful serves and swift volleys a thrilling sight. The score see-sawed as they broke each other's serve.

The final set was nail-biting. Serena was down 5-3. But she wasn't ready to give up. She rallied, her determination palpable in each powerful return. With each point she scored, the crowd held their breath, the tension palpable. And then, after what felt like an eternity, Serena did it. She won the set 7-5, securing her 23rd Grand Slam title.

The crowd erupted into cheers, but the world seemed to stand still for Serena. She had done it. She had made history.

This was more than a victory; it was the pinnacle of Serena's incredible journey - a journey defined by determination, resilience, and an unwavering will to succeed. It wasn't just about the trophy; it was a celebration of Serena, the girl who dreamed big, worked hard, and never gave up.

BETHANY HAMILTON "SOUL SURFER"

As the warm Hawaiian sun bathed the beach on November 16, 2014, at the Women's Pipeline Pro in Oahu, an excited buzz flowed through the crowd. Eyes were drawn to the ocean where a silhouette was taking shape against the morning sky. It was the silhouette of a surfer, not just any surfer, but Bethany Hamilton.

"She's going for it!" Someone shouted. The spectators held their breaths as Bethany positioned herself on her surfboard, a determined look on her face. With her one arm, she skilfully paddled into a huge 9-foot wave, a true beast of nature with a powerful crest and a hollow barrel. Timing it just right, she caught the wave at the perfect moment and stood up, entering the barrel with grace and precision. The tube enclosed around her as she rode it with absolute control, her body perfectly aligned with the curve of the wave. The crowd erupted into a cheer that echoed across the beach as she emerged triumphantly from the barrel, completing one of the most difficult maneuvers in surfing. Her outstanding performance on that particular wave earned her a near-perfect score of 9.7, reflecting her technical excellence and artistry, solidifying her place at the top of the leaderboard in that contest.

In the crowd, Bethany's mother, Cheri Hamilton, watched with a mix of pride and emotion. "That's my girl," she said softly. A tear slipped down her cheek, but it was a tear of joy.

You see, this was not just another surf competition for Bethany. This was her comeback, her victory over a life-altering incident that could have stopped her, but didn't. Hamilton's performance at the Women's Pipeline Pro was the climax of her career. Bethany was back, more determined, more inspiring. She won the contest, proving to the world her unbreakable spirit.

This is the comeback story of Bethany Hamilton.

On February 8, 1990, a baby girl named Bethany Meilani Hamilton was born into the world. Her parents, Tom and Cheri Hamilton, welcomed her with joy and warmth. She was their second child, following her older brothers Noah and Timmy. Little did they know that this island girl would grow up to inspire millions around the world.

Bethany's family lived in the lush paradise of Kauai, Hawaii, a place of shimmering beaches, dazzling waves, and skies painted with brilliant colors each day. From an early age, the ocean became Bethany's playground.

Living in such a paradise had its perks. Tom and Cheri, both surf enthusiasts, nurtured a love for the ocean in their children. Bethany's brothers were her first playmates, and they enjoyed countless days of swimming and building sandcastles. But of all the activities, Bethany's favorite was surfing.

It was almost like the ocean called to her. The way she smiled each time a wave lifted her, you could tell she was home.

"Hey Bethany, ready to catch some waves?" her father would ask. A wide grin would spread across her face, her eyes twinkling with excitement. "You bet, Dad!" she'd reply, a mini surfboard tucked under her arm, ready to tackle the ocean's challenges.

Bethany's parents noticed her knack for surfing early on. Even though she was the smallest on her surfboard, she had a fearless spirit. "Bethany was like a little water sprite," Cheri fondly recalled, "She was never afraid, always eager to take on the next wave."

The warmth and support from her family were crucial in these early years, helping Bethany shape her love for the ocean. Life was all about fun in the sun and riding the waves. This was the blissful world of this little island girl.

Bethany's journey with surfing began when she was barely taller than the surfboard she was learning to balance on. At the tender age of eight, she took to the waves like a dolphin takes to the sea. Her parents, who were both passionate surfers, played a significant role in encouraging her.

One sunny day, her father, Tom, held her little hand and said, "Bethany, the ocean is like life. Sometimes it's calm, sometimes it's wild, but with every wave, there's a ride. All you've got to do is learn to enjoy it." Those words echoed in her mind each time she set foot on her surfboard.

Bethany wasn't just learning to surf; she was forming a bond with the ocean. With every wave she rode, every tumble she took, her connection deepened. The people around started to notice her skills. "Look at that little surfer girl," locals would say. "She's got a natural gift!"

Under the guidance of her parents and the warm Hawaiian sun, Bethany started to transform from an eager novice to a promising young talent. Whether she was practicing her balance on the sandy beach or riding the foam-tipped waves, her passion for surfing could be visibly seen on her smiling face.

Bethany was just nine when her surfing talents started making waves in Kauai's local surf community. In 1995, she entered her first surfing competition, the Rell Sunn Menehune, hosted at the famous Hanalei Bay surf spot. Despite her age and size, Bethany turned heads with her daring moves and fearless spirit. "I'm not afraid of anything! Bring it on!" she'd often say.

At the end of the day, Bethany found herself holding a shiny trophy, beaming with pride. She had not only participated but had won her first surf competition. That was the first among many victories that set her on a path of early surfing success.

At this time, she caught the attention of her future coach, Russell Lewis, a veteran surfer and local legend. Seeing her potential, Russell decided to mentor her. "Bethany, you've got something special," he said to her. "You're fearless. You're determined. You're a born surfer."

Under Russell's guidance, Bethany's skills flourished. Russell taught her more than just techniques. He shared his wisdom about the ocean, the weather, and the art of surfing. He'd often remind her, "The best surfer out there is the one having the most fun." Bethany took those words to heart, and they fueled her journey.

The very next year, at just ten years old, Bethany scored her first sponsorship deal with Rip Curl, a renowned surfwear company. She was over the moon. "I can't believe it! I'm a sponsored surfer!" she said excitedly, holding her new surfboard high above her head.

Bethany's love for surfing and her extraordinary talents were propelling her toward a promising future. But with this success came heightened stakes and tougher competition. Yet, nothing seemed too big for Bethany. She was ready to ride any wave, overcome any challenge. Little did she know then, that the biggest wave of her life was yet to come.

October 31, 2003, started as an ordinary day for Bethany. She was 13 years old and full of life, eager to catch the early morning waves with her best friend, Alana Blanchard, and Alana's father, Holt. They ventured to Tunnels Beach, known for its good surf. However, unbeknownst to them, lurking beneath the deep blue water was a danger nobody anticipated.

As the sun began to rise, Bethany paddled out into the water, her arms working rhythmically against the gentle resistance of the ocean. Suddenly, she felt a powerful tug, and everything changed in an instant. A 14-foot tiger shark had surfaced from the depths and bit down on her left arm. Alana, a few feet away, could only watch in horror.

Despite the excruciating pain, Bethany remained remarkably calm. She remembered thinking, "I gotta get back on my board. I gotta get to the shore." Driven by her sheer will to survive, she managed to paddle back towards the beach with her remaining arm.

Holt Blanchard, Alana's father, immediately sprang into action. Using his knowledge as a lifeguard, he fashioned a tourniquet from a surfboard leash around her bleeding stump, a crucial move that would later be credited with saving her life.

As Bethany was rushed to Wilcox Memorial Hospital, she clung to life, her eyes fixated on the skies. She recalled, "I remember looking at the beautiful Kauai sky and thinking, 'I'm too young to die. I have so many more waves to ride.'" Her determination to survive that dreadful day was as unyielding as the waves she loved to ride.

In that fateful moment, Bethany lost not only her arm but also the appearance of normalcy that her 13-year-old life had held. But what she didn't lose was her unbreakable spirit. As the shark disappeared into the depths from whence it came, it left behind a young girl who was about to embark on an extraordinary journey of resilience and bravery.

After the shark attack, Bethany woke up in a hospital bed, her body weak but her spirit unbroken. With her left arm missing, she felt a part of her identity stripped away. The pain was not only physical; the emotional toll was profound.

Bethany's mother Cheri was by her side, offering words of encouragement and wiping away tears. "Bethany, you are still you, and you're stronger than you think," she said, her hand firmly clutching Bethany's.

Her father Tom echoed these sentiments, "Bethany, you've conquered bigger waves. This is just another one, and you'll ride it out, too." Their unwavering support was a beacon of hope for Bethany during those tough times.

Despite the immense support, the road to recovery was filled with challenges. Bethany wrestled with bouts of depression and anxiety. She would often sit at the beach, watching the waves that once brought joy, now a reminder of the tragic incident.

But it was in these depths of despair that Bethany found strength in her faith. She believed her life was spared for a reason, and she clung onto this belief. Bethany was quoted saying, "I don't need easy, I just need possible. The Lord will carry me through."

Bethany was also surrounded by her church community, who prayed with her, encouraged her, and helped her see the light at the end of the tunnel. The love and support she received played a crucial role in lifting her spirits and fuelling her determination to recover.

While this chapter in Bethany's life was marked by struggle and pain, it was also a testament to her unyielding spirit and unwavering faith. Despite the tumultuous waves of adversity, Bethany refused to let her spirit sink. She chose to swim, to fight, and to live. She was on her way to recovery, inching closer to the waves she yearned to ride once again.

Just a month after the shark attack, Bethany made a decision that shocked everyone. With a determined glint in her eye, she announced, "I'm going back to the water." And true to her word, she did.

On a cool morning in December 2023, Bethany approached the surf, her heart beating in rhythm with the crashing waves. There was fear, but it was overshadowed by her unyielding resolve. As she paddled out into the water with her father, the ocean seemed to welcome her back, gentle waves lapping against her surfboard.

To the amazement of all who watched, Bethany managed to ride the waves once again, her face radiant with joy. However, it was not without challenges. With only one arm, she had to learn to balance differently, paddle differently, and even pop up onto the board differently. But she was nothing if not adaptable.

"I've got to be clever," she said. "I might have one arm, but my mind is still intact." And clever she was. Bethany, despite losing her arm in a shark attack, didn't let her disability stop her from surfing. To adapt to her unique situation, her father customized her surfboard by installing a handle in the center of the board. This modification was crucial as it enabled Bethany to duck dive under waves more efficiently. By holding onto the handle, she could maneuver her board underwater, which is an essential skill for navigating through large waves.

Yet, as she returned to competitive surfing, she faced a new kind of wave, a wave of skepticism. Some doubted her ability to compete with two-handed surfers. Some viewed her as a sympathy case. But Bethany wasn't interested in sympathy. She was there to compete, to do what she loved most, to surf.

"I'm not surfing to prove anything to anyone," she declared. "I'm surfing because I love it. I'm surfing because it's part of who I am." Bethany's unbroken spirit not only got her back on the surfboard but also back in the competition.

As Bethany cut through the towering waves, she was not just a one-armed surfer; she was a beacon of resilience, a testament to the power of determination.

Bethany's return to professional surfing was no small feat, but she was determined to ride the waves of success. In 2004, just a year after the shark attack, Bethany astounded the world by winning the National Scholastic Surfing Association (NSSA) national championship, a testament to her unbreakable spirit.

Bethany was making waves in the surfing world, but she also faced formidable opponents, which included competitive surfers like Lakey Peterson and Malia Manuel. Bethany didn't see these rivals as threats; instead, they fueled her determination to improve.

One of Bethany's memorable quotes from this period was, "I don't need to beat them. I need to be my best. Every wave I catch, every trick I land, is a victory for me." True to her words, Bethany focused on bettering herself, pushing her limits, and achieving her personal best in every competition.

One big setback was failing to qualify for the World Surf League (WSL) in 2010. But true to her resilient spirit, Bethany didn't see these setbacks as failures; she saw them as stepping stones towards success.

She once told a reporter, "You know, the ocean doesn't always give you the wave you want. Sometimes, you wipe out. But then you get back on your board, and you catch the next wave. Life's like that, too."

Bethany's journey in professional surfing was filled with remarkable victories and daunting challenges. Just a year after her comeback from the shark attack, she claimed victory at the National Scholastic Surfing Association (NSSA) National Championships on June 26, 2004, announcing her return in grand style. Her triumphs continued as she won the O'Neill Island Girl Junior Pro in the Philippines in October 2005 and later proved her expertise in big wave surfing by conquering the T&C Women's Pipeline Championships in Hawaii on February 16, 2007.

In the climax of her career, Bethany soared to victory at the Surf n Sea Pipeline Women's Pro on March 11, 2014, a contest held at one of the most iconic surf spots in the world. Her remarkable performance as runner-up in the 2014 Fiji Women's Pro further garnered worldwide attention, cementing her status as a force in professional surfing.

In July 2016, her courage, determination, and athletic excellence were honored with an ESPY Award for Best Female Athlete with a Disability.

Beyond the crashing waves and the thrill of surfing, Bethany Hamilton was making a difference on dry land, too. Her story of resilience and faith had captured the hearts of millions, and she harnessed this influence to inspire others and give back to the community.

Bethany became a motivational speaker, sharing her story with audiences worldwide. From school assemblies to global conferences, she spoke about the power of resilience, faith, and determination.

She also penned a best-selling autobiography, "Soul Surfer", in 2004, which was later adapted into a successful movie. The book and the movie shared her journey of overcoming adversity and made her an inspiration for many around the world.

Bethany's philanthropic efforts included working with organizations like Friends of Bethany, which supports shark attack survivors and amputees. Her desire to give back to the community showed another aspect of her strength—her compassion and her big heart.

But amidst all her endeavors, Bethany cherished her role as a wife and mother the most. In 2013, she married Adam Dirks, a youth minister. Throughout her pregnancy, Bethany Hamilton devoted up to five hours each day to surfing in order to maintain her fitness. Given that even losing an arm didn't deter her from surfing, it was clear that carrying a baby wouldn't either.

On the 1st of June, 2015, Bethany and Adam were overjoyed to welcome their firstborn, Tobias, into the world.

She shared her love for the ocean with her family and was often spotted teaching her sons to surf.

Bethany Hamilton was more than just a surfer. She was a beacon of hope, a loving wife and mother, a philanthropist, a writer, and an inspiration to many. She proved that one could go beyond personal challenges and make a positive impact on the lives of others. Her story was a testament to the power of the human spirit, which refuses to be broken and continues to thrive and make waves, both in the ocean and in the hearts of the people she inspires.

MICHAEL JORDAN "AIR JORDAN"

The final seconds of Game 6 in the 1998 NBA Finals, and the crowd's roar shakes the arena. Michael Jordan, 35, has one shot to secure the Chicago Bulls' sixth championship in eight years. The tension is as thick as his favorite Chicago deep-dish pizza. Utah Jazz fans cheer, the scoreboard too close for comfort. Jordan dribbles, sweat pouring down his face, his legs aching but his eyes fixed on the hoop. "Failure? Sure, I've failed," he thinks to himself, remembering his years of practice and past defeats, "But not trying? Never." This game, this moment, is a culmination of everything Michael has worked for, and it's all on the line. He knows it, feels it, and is ready to face it.

His eyes dart around the court, mind whirling faster than his feet. A faint chant grows among the crowd, "Jordan! Jordan! Jordan!" It fuels him, the familiar rhythm of his name echoing in his ears. The ball is part of him, an extension of his will. He is reminded of his father's words, "Michael, you can do anything you set your mind to. You just have to believe." And with that belief, he leaps, pushing through the air as time seems to freeze.

His opponent, Bryon Russell of the Utah Jazz, tries to block him, but Michael is relentless, sidestepping Russell with a swift, practiced movement that speaks of years of dedication and tireless practice.

Then, he releases the ball. For a moment, everything stands still. The world watches, breath held, as the ball sails through the air, spins, and – swoosh – sinks into the net. The crowd erupts, and the stadium shakes with the deafening roars of fans.

As the cheers echo around him, Michael Jordan stands still, a calm smile spreading across his face. His shot is a message, not just to the Jazz, but to everyone who dared to dream, to aspire, to rise above adversity. he did, showing the world what it truly means to be like 'Air Jordan'.

February 17, 1963, in the heart of Brooklyn, New York, on a chilly winter day, a baby boy named Michael Jeffrey Jordan was born. Little did anyone know that this small, wailing infant was destined to become one of the greatest basketball players in history.

Growing up in a bustling household with four siblings - two brothers and two sisters - Michael quickly learned to fight for his place, especially against his competitive older brother Larry. He once said, "My brother Larry used to beat me up in one-on-one basketball games. But each time he won, it only made me work harder."

James and Deloris Jordan, Michael's parents, were a vital part of his journey. His father, James, worked at an electric plant, and his mother, Deloris, worked at a bank. They both believed in hard work and taught their children to do the same.

One summer day, Michael's dad built a basketball hoop behind their small brick house. It wasn't perfect, but it was theirs. Michael spent hours shooting at the makeshift hoop, the clang of the ball hitting the rim echoing through the evening. One day, he missed shot after shot, and his frustration grew. Seeing this, his dad walked over and said, "Son, you're focusing on what you're doing wrong. Look at what you can improve, and keep trying." Those words stuck with Michael, shaping the way he viewed challenges and setbacks.

For Michael Jordan, the path to basketball started with a sibling rivalry and a bumpy, well-worn court. His older brother, Larry, was always there, just a step ahead, a bit taller, a bit better. But young Michael wasn't about to be left in the dust. He once said, "My older brother Larry was my biggest competition. We'd fight like crazy over our games. He was better than me too. But when I beat him that one time? I knew I could play this game."

Their duels on the makeshift basketball court behind their house were epic. No matter how many times Larry won, Michael would bounce right back, ready for another round. This rivalry not only fueled his love for basketball but also sparked the fiery competitiveness we'd come to associate with Michael Jordan.

Michael's relentless drive wasn't limited to his backyard court. In school, he was seen as talented but raw, and his dream of becoming a basketball superstar seemed distant. There were days filled with gruelling practice, battling against players who were naturally gifted, struggling to keep pace. But what he lacked in natural ability, he made up for with an unwavering commitment to improve.

In junior high, he joined the school's basketball team, where the challenges mounted. Opposing teams were tough, and Michael often found himself struggling to stand out. He was benched in crucial games and faced criticism for his playing style. But through every failure, the spark in his eyes never dimmed. He would watch game tapes, spend extra hours on the court, and even seek help from local college players, all in pursuit of refining his skills.

Michael's journey wasn't without its hurdles. Imagine a 15-year-old Michael, awkward and gangly, standing in a hallway of Emsley A. Laney High School. His eyes scan the list pinned on the notice board, searching for his name under the varsity basketball team. But his name isn't there. He's been cut from the team. Michael recalled, "It was embarrassing not making that team. They posted the roster and it was there for a long, long time without my name on it. I remember being really mad, too, because there was a guy who made it that really wasn't as good as me."

The disappointment stung, but it didn't break him. If anything, it fueled his determination to work even harder.

He spent that summer playing junior varsity basketball, growing four inches, and practicing tirelessly, letting his disappointment fuel his determination.

When 18-year-old Michael Jordan walked onto the gorgeous campus of the University of North Carolina, he carried with him a fiery ambition and a dream to become one of the greatest.

Under the guidance of the legendary coach Dean Smith, a whole new world opened up for Michael. Coach Smith wasn't just a mentor; he was a guiding force who believed in Michael, pushing him to aim higher and work harder. "Coach Smith taught me how to play basketball, but more than that, he taught me about life," Michael would often say.

In 1982, the NCAA Championship game between the North Carolina Tar Heels and Georgetown Hoyas was in full swing. The clock was ticking down, and the Tar Heels were down by one point. The ball was passed to Michael, then a freshman. It was his chance to make a difference, to tip the scales in their favor.

He could hear his heart pounding in his chest, feel the sweat trickling down his face. The crowd was a sea of noise, but he blocked it all out, focusing on the hoop. He took the shot. The ball whooshed through the air and swished into the net, scoring the winning points for the Tar Heels.

That game-winning shot did more than just secure the championship for the Tar Heels; it announced Michael Jordan to the world. It showed everyone that here was a young man who could keep his cool under pressure, who had the grit to take the last shot, who could be relied on when the game was on the line.

College years were transformative for Michael. He left North Carolina not just with a degree in geography but with invaluable lessons, lifelong friendships, and a reputation as a clutch player.

In the summer of 1984, with the Chicago skyline as a backdrop, a fresh-faced 21-year-old stepped onto the NBA stage. The third overall pick by the Chicago Bulls in the NBA draft, Michael Jordan was about to embark on a new adventure, one that would change the face of basketball forever.

As a rookie, Michael hit the ground running. With his thrilling dunks and acrobatic plays, he quickly became a crowd favorite. The fans weren't the only ones impressed; his performance also caught the eyes of the experts. He once fondly remembered, "They didn't think a kid like me could make it in the pros. But I was determined to prove them wrong."

And prove them wrong he did! By the end of his first season, Michael had won the hearts of fans and critics alike, being named NBA Rookie of the Year.

But the road to greatness was not without bumps. In his second season, disaster struck. Michael broke his foot in a game against the Golden State Warriors. It was a crushing setback, and it sidelined him for 64 games.

"I remember lying there, looking at my foot, thinking, 'Is this it? Is my career over?'"

But Michael was no stranger to adversity. He knew this was just another obstacle he needed to overcome. He poured all his energy into his recovery, fighting his way back to the court with the same determination that had earned him a place in the NBA.

When he returned to the game, he was more formidable than ever. He went on to win seven consecutive scoring titles, dazzling fans and opponents alike with his unique blend of speed, agility, and precision.

"Sometimes, things may not go your way, but the effort should be there every single night," Michael would say. And true to his words, he consistently put in the effort, turning challenges into stepping-stones, and continually raising the bar for himself and others. The young man from North Carolina, who was once cut from his high school team, had not only made it to the NBA but was well on his way to becoming a legend.

The 1980s was a time of transformation for the NBA, and at the center of this change was a young man who seemed to defy gravity. Michael Jordan, affectionately known as 'Air Jordan', was not only playing basketball; he was redefining it.

Every time Michael took to the court, the anticipation in the air was electric. Fans packed into arenas, eyes wide and hearts pounding, waiting for the magic to unfold. And Michael didn't disappoint. He would run, leap, and twist in mid-air, performing feats that seemed impossible. His dunks weren't just shots; they were spectacles that left fans and rivals alike in awe. "Every time I took flight," he once said, "I wanted to do something special, something memorable."

His high-flying style of play quickly gained him popularity and this is where his nickname, 'Air Jordan', was cemented.

But Michael was not content with just flashy moves and personal glory. He understood that basketball was a team sport, and individual brilliance meant little without team success. "Talent wins games, but teamwork and intelligence win championships," he often emphasized.

In 1988, Michael's growing understanding of team play, coupled with his personal dominance on the court, led to him being awarded his first NBA Most Valuable Player (MVP) award. But there was more to his game than just scoring; Michael was also a ferocious defender, winning the NBA Defensive Player of the Year in the same year.

His defensive prowess was often overshadowed by his scoring, but it was equally important in crafting the legend of 'Air Jordan.'

In the summer of 1993, at the peak of his career, Michael Jordan was hit with a devastating blow. His father, James Jordan, who had been his rock and guiding light, was tragically taken from him. The news sent shockwaves through Michael's world. He once said, "My father used to say that it's never too late to do anything you wanted to do. He was my best friend, my mentor, my confidant."

The bond between Michael and his father was special. James had not just nurtured Michael's love for basketball but also instilled in him values of hard work, determination, and resilience. Michael's every victory, every leap, every trophy, had been shared with his father. Now, the game that brought them together was a painful reminder of his loss.

In an unexpected move, Michael decided to step away from basketball. "I'm at peace with myself. My father saw my last game, and that means a lot," he told reporters during his retirement announcement. His decision left fans and players alike stunned. But for Michael, it was a time to grieve, reflect, and seek solace.

In this challenging phase, he found an unlikely refuge: baseball, a game his father had loved and they had often played together. Switching sports was not easy, and many questioned his decision. But Michael was composed. As he put it, "I wanted to follow my heart. I wanted to honor my father."

Playing for the Birmingham Barons, a minor league team, Michael showed his resilience. He wasn't the best baseball player, but he gave it his all, demonstrating the same dedication and hard work he had in basketball. He remembered, "Every day in the field, I could feel my dad cheering me on. That's all I needed."

Michael's journey through personal loss taught him valuable lessons about resilience and the power of following your heart.

Michael Jordan's time away from basketball was a period of healing, reflection, and growth. By 1995, whispers began to circulate that Michael might return to the court. And just like a well-plotted thriller, on March 18, 1995, he announced his comeback with a simple yet powerful statement: "I'm back."

On returning to the Chicago Bulls, Michael brought with him a renewed vigor, a sense of purpose, and a greater appreciation for the game he loved. His time away had only made him hungrier. I never lost my love for the game; I just found a new perspective."

With Michael back, the Bulls were once again a force to reckon with. He led them to an unprecedented "three-peat" from 1996 to 1998, winning three consecutive NBA championships. Michael was no longer just a player; he was a leader, guiding and pushing his team to reach new heights.

The 1998 NBA Finals against the Utah Jazz was the ultimate test of his resilience and mental toughness. He glanced at the clock; the pressure was mounting. Standing before him was Bryon Russell, determined to block his path. Michael dribbled, feinted, then pushed off slightly, creating just enough space. Michael took the final shot. "I've missed more than 9000 shots in my career... but I've learned that every failure is a step towards success. At that moment, all I had was the ball, the basket, and a will to win."

With 5.2 seconds left on the clock, he let the ball fly. And like a story coming full circle, Michael's last shot as a Bull found its mark, sealing their victory. His teammates, the crowd, the world watched in awe as Michael Jordan, the boy who had been cut from his high school team, stood as a champion, defining an era of basketball.

After his memorable stint with the Bulls, Michael Jordan surprised the world again by announcing his retirement. But basketball was in his blood, and he wasn't away for long. In 2000, he joined the Washington Wizards as an executive and part-owner. The office was a different game, and Michael brought his competitive spirit and strategic mind to it. But he couldn't stay off the court for long.

In 2001, at the age of 38, he made another return to the game, this time as a player for the Wizards. Many wondered, "Can he still play?" Michael answered with his actions. His first game back, he scored 19 points, reminding everyone of the old magic. He remarked, "Age is just a number. It's all about the love of the game."

Playing for the Wizards was different. He was older, surrounded by younger players, and the team wasn't as strong as the Bulls. But Michael saw it as a challenge and an opportunity to mentor the young team. He often said, "Talent wins games, but teamwork wins championships." He was no longer just a player; he was a mentor, guiding and pushing the young team, teaching them the value of hard work, determination, and resilience.

After two seasons with the Wizards, he retired for the final time in 2003. His departure marked the end of an era, but his influence on the game was far from over.

His legacy goes beyond his six championships, five MVP awards, or his induction into the Basketball Hall of Fame. It is found in the hearts of countless fans, the players he inspired, and the next generation who continue to wear the number 23.

And so, his legacy lives on, just like his famous free-throw line dunk, suspended in time, reminding us all to keep aiming high, to keep pushing, and to always, always believe in our dreams.

USAIN BOLT
"LIGHTNING BOLT"

"Ready, set, BANG!" The starting gun echoed across the Beijing National Stadium in 2008. As if jolted by the crack of thunder, a man burst forward, his long strides eating up the track like a cheetah in full chase. His name was Usain Bolt, and he was about to make history.

The spectators gaped as Bolt crossed the finish line, a blur of black, gold, and green—the colors of his beloved Jamaica. The massive digital clock blinked 9.69 seconds, a new world record. The crowd erupted in a deafening cheer as Bolt danced with joy, electrifying the stadium with his infectious energy.

Are you ready for a thrilling race through time to discover the starting line of this spectacular sprinting sensation?

Usain Bolt was born on August 21, 1986, in the small town of Sherwood Content, Jamaica. From a young age, he was full of energy, always running and playing. His mom, Jennifer, says he was always on the move as soon as he could walk. He would often race the local dogs and even the wind!

Bolt's dad, Wellesley, owned a local grocery shop where Bolt would often help. He saw it as his training ground and would race to deliver groceries to customers His sister, Sherine, would stand at the shop's entrance, watching him vanish into the distance. Nobody could ever catch him, not even the quickest local dogs that sometimes joined the chase.

Growing up in Sherwood Content, Bolt's life was simple but filled with love, laughter, and lots and lots of running. It was these early years that helped shape him into the amazing sprinter the world would come to know.

Bolt's family was not rich by any means. Their home in Sherwood Content was modest, nestled between lush green hills and winding dirt paths. The wooden walls had seen years of weather, but inside, the house was filled with warmth and joy.

He was nurtured by the love and wisdom of his parents, Jennifer and Wellesley, who taught him life's most important lessons. His parents, honest and hardworking people, were his first role models.

His father, a lover of sports himself, taught Bolt the value of determination.

One sunny afternoon, after Bolt had lost a race to a friend, he found himself sulking under a shady tree. His father approached, a soft smile playing on his lips.

"Remember son," he said, kneeling down and looking into young Bolt's teary eyes, "the race is long. It's not always about who runs fastest but who keeps running. Look at the river; it doesn't rush but still reaches the sea."

Bolt looked up, the words sinking in. The disappointment began to fade, replaced by a new understanding. Those simple words stuck with him, becoming his mantra, shaping his attitude towards racing

At age 6, Usain started school at Waldensia Primary, a small school in Falmouth. Tucked away in one of the poorer areas of Sherwood, the building showed signs of wear, with peeling paint and creaking wooden floors. Desks and chairs were old and mismatched, but the place was filled with dedicated teachers and lively students. Despite its humble appearance, it was here that Usain's passion for running began to flourish.

At the school's annual sports day, an eight-year-old Bolt lined up for his first race. As the race began, he experienced the rush of adrenaline, the wind on his face, and the blur of the ground beneath his feet. These sensations would become familiar and cherished to him - it was the thrill of the race.

From then on, every chance he got, he ran. Whether it was in the school playground or on the streets of Sherwood Content, Bolt was always on his feet, racing against time, his friends, and sometimes, even and even the rumbling trains that couldn't keep up with him!

Bolt was a natural, and his talent did not go unnoticed. Mr. McNeil, his Physical Education teacher, saw the potential in Bolt's quick feet and guided him. He was Bolt's first mentor, shaping his raw talent and teaching him the basics of sprinting. Mr. McNeil would say, "Usain, running is not just about speed. It's about technique and stamina. Always remember that."

Under Mr. McNeil's guidance, Bolt trained harder. His day started early and he started running at 6 in the morning, then, during breaks and also after school, each time pushing himself a little more. Running was no longer just a game. It was a goal, a challenge, a dream.

As he grew older, Bolt started participating in local races. His first major race was the Trelawny Parish Championship. As he stood at the starting line, Bolt felt a familiar rush of adrenaline. He heard the whistle, and he was off, chasing the wind. When he crossed the finish line, he was not just the fastest in his school, but in his entire district!

His victory made people sit up and take notice. His parents, his friends, his teachers, everyone began to see the budding champion in him. Bolt was no longer just the quick kid from Sherwood Content. He was a young athlete, a sprinter with a promising future.

The next chapter of this adventure began when he joined William Knibb Memorial High School.

At William Knibb, Bolt initially saw himself as a cricket player. He adored the sport and showed great promise as a fast bowler. However, his cricket coach, noticing Bolt's exceptional speed on the field, had other ideas.

"Bolt," he said one day after practice, "ever thought about giving track and field a try?"

This suggestion took Bolt by surprise. He loved running, but cricket held a special place in his heart. However, trusting his coach's judgement, Bolt decided to give it a shot.

Joining the track and field team, Bolt started training with a renewed sense of focus and dedication. The cricket pitch gave way to the running track, and the cricket ball was replaced by running spikes. His speed and natural talent made him stand out, even amongst the older and more experienced athletes. Under his coach's strict yet supportive guidance, Bolt blossomed.

In his early teens, Bolt had begun to make waves on the international athletics scene. His unique combination of height, power, and speed was attracting attention, and people were starting to talk about the lightning-fast boy from Jamaica.

His breakout moment came at the 2002 World Junior Championships in Kingston, Jamaica. Bolt was just fifteen, the youngest on the team, but he was undeterred. "Age is just a number," he would say, "What matters is how fast you run."

With the world watching, Bolt lined up against the fastest juniors from across the globe. He felt the nerves, but as he crouched on the starting line, a calmness washed over him. The whistle blew, and Bolt shot off like a bullet, his tall figure slicing through the air. He crossed the finish line in first place, creating history by becoming the youngest junior gold medalist ever. Bolt had officially announced his arrival on the world stage.

However, the journey to the top is rarely smooth. Bolt's rapid ascent was slowed by a series of injuries that forced him off the tracks and onto the sidelines. His unique running style, a result of his 6'5" height, put immense strain on his body, causing him to suffer painful injuries, one severe hamstring strain and a further strain to his lower back. Doubts crept in. Would he ever reach his full potential? Could his body withstand the pressures of high-speed running?

He dedicated himself to healing and strengthening his body. He spent long hours in physiotherapy, conditioning his muscles, and learning to adapt his running style to minimize injury risks.

Through this period of adversity, Bolt learned some of life's toughest lessons. He learned that success is not just about winning races but also about overcoming obstacles.

At eighteen, Bolt moved to the capital, Kingston to train with Glen Mills, a renowned coach with a reputation for creating champions. Mills saw in Bolt the raw power of untamed lightning and took it upon himself to guide this extraordinary talent.

The training sessions were intense. Coach Mills had a mantra, "It's all about the hard work. You've got to put in the time if you want to see the results." Bolt's days started early and ended late, filled with drills, workouts, and endless laps around the track.

Mills focused not only on Bolt's physical strength but also on his mental toughness. Bolt was taught to envision his success before every race, to feel the wind against his face, the rush of crossing the finish line. Mills believed, "It's not just about the body. It's also about the mind. Train your mind, and the body will follow."

Mills also helped Bolt improve his start—a weakness in his earlier races like all tall sprinters. With Mills' guidance, Bolt perfected his 'drive phase', the first few crucial seconds of the race. His starts were now explosive, giving him an early advantage that he would often turn into commanding leads.

In these years under Mills' mentorship, Bolt's unique running style was refined, and his confidence solidified. The countless hours on the track, the sweat, the pain, the exhaustion—it all came together, turning Bolt into an athlete unlike any the world had seen before. The bolt was unleashed.

One memorable training session, Mills was working closely with him on improving his speed. That afternoon, they were at the University of the West Indies track. His coach had seen him run fast, but this time was different. As Bolt sprinted down the track, Mills glanced at his stopwatch, unable to believe the time he was seeing: 10. 3 seconds for a 100-meter dash! He shook the device, tapped it, and looked again. The numbers hadn't changed. Bolt had just run a mind-boggling time, so fast that Mills initially thought his stopwatch had to be broken! This moment marked one of the many times Bolt's speed would leave those around him in disbelief.

The year 2008 was a defining moment in Bolt's career. The world stage was set - the Beijing Olympics. Bolt, now a fierce competitor on the international stage, was ready to make his mark.

In the lead-up to the games, Bolt trained like never before. His coach Mills motivated him by saying, "You have the lightning, Usain. Now let the thunder roar!" Bolt internalized these words and turned them into action. Every morning, he woke up with one thought in mind - the Olympics.

Bolt arrived in Beijing amidst much speculation. His performance in the Olympic trials had been impressive, but the world wondered if the young Jamaican could maintain his form on the ultimate stage.

Among his main rivals was Tyson Gay, the American sprinter who had the fastest times of the year. Bolt respected his competitors, but he did not fear them. He believed in his abilities and knew that if he ran his race, he could triumph.

Bolt's first event was the 100 meters. As he stepped onto the track, his heart pounded with excitement and a bit of nerves. Looking at the crowd, he remembered his journey, his family, his coach, and all the hard work he had put into reaching this point. He was ready.

Bolt exploded out of the blocks. The world watched in awe as he surged down the track, every stride pulling him further from his rivals. He crossed the finish line in a stunning 9.69 seconds, shattering the world record. Bolt had done more than just win; he had dominated. The thunder had indeed roared!

Days later, Bolt lined up for the 200 meters, an event close to his heart. With the confidence of his 100 meters victory, Bolt raced like the wind, crossing the finish line in a world record time of 19.30 seconds. The double gold was his, and the world was astounded.

Bolt had arrived at the Olympics as a promising sprinter and left as a global superstar. The young boy from the Jamaican countryside had achieved his dream, becoming the world's fastest man. The thunder had roared in Beijing, and Usain Bolt was the storm.

The world had marveled at Bolt's performance in Beijing. Yet, a new challenge loomed on the horizon—the 2012 London Olympics. Bolt knew that staying at the top would be harder than getting there. However, he was determined to prove that lightning could indeed strike twice.

The four years following Beijing were not easy. Bolt was dealing with an increasing pressure to perform and the high expectations of millions around the world. There was also a growing list of rising sprinters eager to dethrone him. Tyson Gay from the United States, Yohan Blake from Jamaica, and Asafa Powell, also from Jamaica. These guys were no slouches, and they were hungry to beat the Bolt.

However, Bolt's attitude was unwavering. He said, "Pressure is something you feel when you don't know what you're doing. I know what I'm doing." He took the challenges in his stride, channeling the pressure into an intense focus on his training.

Bolt stuck to his regimen with an ironclad resolve. He spent hours on the track, refining his technique, and strengthening his body. He was often the first to arrive at training and the last to leave.

He also worked on his mental game. Bolt visualized himself winning, the feel of the gold medal against his chest, the sound of the crowd cheering his name. He knew the importance of a strong mindset and was not leaving anything to chance.

As the London Olympics approached, Bolt was ready. He had worked tirelessly, sacrificed much, and faced every challenge with a smile and his signature "lightning bolt" pose. He stepped onto the London track with a single goal—to show the world that he was still the fastest.

In London, Bolt again rose to the occasion. He won the 100 meters and 200 meters, just as he had in Beijing, breaking his own records and dazzling the world with his speed and charisma. Bolt had done it—he had struck twice.

Then came the most unforgettable moment of his entire career—a moment that would define greatness, defy odds, and dazzle the world. A moment that young athletes would aspire to, and legends would look back on with respect.

On August 16, 2009, in Berlin's iconic Olympiastadion, something extraordinary was about to happen. Usain Bolt, a 6'5" sprinter from the small town of Sherwood Content, Jamaica, was standing on the brink of history, ready to shatter the very boundaries of human speed.

Bolt, wearing his signature golden spikes, stepped to the line, his eyes locked on the track ahead. Beside him stood fierce competitors like Tyson Gay and Asafa Powell, their faces masked with concentration, eyes also on the prize. The silence was overwhelming as the runners took their marks.

The gun cracked, and the runners exploded off the line. Tyson Gay, one of Bolt's greatest competitors, was the first to react, but Bolt was right on his heels. Bolt's signature stride emerged as he edged passed Tyson and started to pull away from the pack. Arms and legs in unison, his muscles where machine-like, mind and body perfectly in sync. A force that seemed otherworldly, his acceleration ignited the crowd's roar.

The other runners strained, but Bolt's face remained focused. Gay was close behind, his body pushing to its limit, but Bolt was already setting a new standard, showing the world the true meaning of sprinting supremacy.

By the midpoint of the race, his lead was clear. The crowd, on its feet, was a sea of faces, eyes wide, a shared realization of witnessing history. Bolt's legs were a blur; his arms drove him onward, his entire being focused on that finish line.

As Powell began to fall behind, Gay pushed harder. Yet Bolt was in his own world now, running not just to win but to defy the very limits of what was humanly possible. Approaching the end, a triumphant smile broke across Bolt's face. The roar of the crowd reached a deafening pitch.

Bolt crossed the line, arms outstretched, the stadium erupting.

As Bolt crossed the line, arms outstretched, the stadium erupted in pure, unbridled joy.

The time flashed on the giant screen: 9.58 seconds.

A collective gasp swept through the crowd, followed by an even louder cheer.

"NINE POINT FIVE EIGHT! SMASHING THE WORLD RECORED! UNBELIEVABLE! He's done it again! Usain Bolt has broken his own world record"

The commentators voice resonated in the hearts of every spectator, adding to the wave of emotion sweeping across the stands.

Facing the crowd, he bent one arm at the elbow, his fingers mimicking a lightning bolt, the other arm outstretched behind him. The stadium went wild, cameras flashing, capturing this iconic moment. The "Lightning Bolt" pose, as unforgettable as the man himself

In 2017, Bolt retired after a great career. His last race was in London and it was very emotional. But retirement was just a new start for him. He became a mentor and started a foundation to help young people in Jamaica. Bolt has left a big mark on the world of athletics, not just with his records, but also with his work off the track. He inspires people to dream big and work hard

The boy who loved to run, the man who became a world champion, and the legend who taught us to chase our dreams.

LEWIS HAMILTON "HAMMER TIME"

As the last lap of the 2008 Brazilian Grand Prix thundered into life, 23-year-old Lewis Hamilton was sitting at the wheel of his McLaren racing car, while his heart was racing in his chest. His dream of becoming the youngest World Champion in Formula One history was about to come true. But the race hadn't been easy, and this ending was even trickier. It was a cloudy day at the Interlagos racetrack, with the rain playing hide and seek, adding to the mounting tension.

"In the cockpit of a racing car, you don't have much time to think, but in moments like these, your whole life flashes before your eyes," Lewis later shared. The race was as unpredictable as a rollercoaster ride. With the rain pouring down, Hamilton found himself in sixth place, one position away from the championship glory he yearned for.

With just a few corners left in the race, his car roared past Timo Glock's slowing Toyota, and he secured the fifth position he needed. The crowd erupted in cheers. Lewis had won the World Championship! As he crossed the finish line, the young champion's voice crackled over the team radio, filled with pure joy, 'I can't believe it! Thank you, thank you!' His voice conveyed the joy of a dream realized, a culmination of years of dedication and hard work."

This day in 2008, when Hamilton clinched his first World Championship title, marked a pivotal moment in his life. But, to truly understand the magnitude of this victory, we need to hit the rewind button.

On a cool January day in 1985, a star was born in the quiet town of Stevenage, England. His parents, Carmen and Anthony, named him Lewis Carl Hamilton. The Hamilton household was modest, but filled with love. Lewis's parents separated when he was just two years old, and he lived with his mother and half-sisters until he was twelve

It was his father, Anthony, who noticed the spark in his son. Anthony was a man of humble beginnings, working multiple jobs to support his family. Despite the hardships, he believed in nurturing Lewis's passion. "He was always interested in cars," Anthony recalled. "As a child, he would sit in front of the TV, completely absorbed in car racing shows."

This shared love for racing brought Lewis and his father closer. Their bond was as strong as steel, yet as tender as a lullaby. The young boy looked up to his father as his hero, his mentor. "My dad always seemed to know everything about cars and racing," Lewis would often say. "He was my superhero."

On Christmas morning in 1991, six-year-old Lewis received a gift that would change his life—a remote-control car. It wasn't just a toy for Lewis; it was the steering wheel to his dreams.

"It was love at first sight," Lewis would recall with a twinkle in his eye. "The moment I held that controller in my hands, I knew this was what I wanted to do." His infectious enthusiasm was impossible to ignore. As his little car zoomed around the living room, Lewis's dreams began to race too.

Lewis Hamilton's talent for racing caught his father Anthony's eye early on. He brought Lewis to a radio-controlled car racing club in Stevenage, where his abilities astonished onlookers. Lewis, the club's youngest participant, exhibited the focus and precision of a seasoned racer.

"He raced like a professional," Anthony recalled, "mastering racing lines and handling even the trickiest situations."

Lewis's adventures with his remote-control car didn't just end with local races. At just eight years old, he became the British Radio Controlled Car Association champion. This feat was impressive for a boy his age. But Lewis, with a sparkle in his eyes and his dream in his heart, had just begun.

"I remember winning my first race," Lewis said. "I was this tiny kid with a controller, standing on a box so I could see the track. Winning that day didn't just give me a trophy. It gave me the belief that I could race, and one day, I would race real cars."

Lewis told his father, "Dad, I want to race real cars! I want to go fast!" Seeing his son's talent, he promised Lewis, "If you work hard at school and give your best in everything you do, I'll find a way to support your dream." This promise marked a turning point in Lewis's life, steering him towards a future in racing.

"Hey, Lewis, do you remember what I promised you?" Anthony Hamilton asked his son one day, his eyes twinkling. Eight-year-old Lewis looked at his father, his heart pounding with anticipation. "You said if I did well in school, you'd help me race real cars," Lewis replied. Anthony broke into a broad smile, and there it was - Lewis's first go-kart.

That day marked the beginning of Lewis's journey into the world of karting. No longer confined to the restrictions of a remote controller, Lewis was finally behind the wheel, the roar of the engine filling his ears, the rush of speed coursing through his veins. He was right where he wanted to be - in the driver's seat.

Learning to handle the go-kart was like learning a new language for Lewis. But he was a quick study. He spent countless hours practicing, each lap making him faster, sharper, and more confident. "I fell in love with the speed, the control, the feeling of being one with the machine," Lewis said, remembering his early karting days. "It was the most alive I had ever felt."

Lewis started racing competitively, with his father cheering him on. His big break came when he won the British Kart Championship at only ten years old. But there were also challenges. Sometimes he'd skid or make mistakes, but this didn't stop him. He once said, "Every time I fell, I learnt something new. Every time I lost, I found a new reason to win."

Every racing enthusiast knew the name Ron Dennis. He was the boss of McLaren, one of the biggest teams in Formula One. Imagine the thrill when a ten-year-old Lewis Hamilton found out he was going to meet this legend at an awards ceremony.

"I remember being so nervous," Lewis shared. "But my dad had always taught me to believe in myself, to chase my dreams no matter how big they seemed." So, he mustered the courage, walked up to Ron Dennis, and held out his hand.

"Mr. Dennis, my name is Lewis Hamilton. One day, I'm going to race for you," Lewis said, looking straight into the eyes of the surprised McLaren boss. Dennis, taken aback by the young boy's audacity and confidence, wrote in his autograph, "Phone me in nine years, and we'll sort something out then."

This story is a key part of Lewis's journey, showing his determination and high ambitions. After promising himself and Ron Dennis that he would race for him, Lewis focused even more on his racing. "Every time I got in my kart, I remembered my promise to Ron," said Lewis. "It wasn't just about winning races now, it was about making my dream come true."

Ron Dennis watched Lewis's progress closely. He saw his talent and his determination to succeed. He knew that Lewis would keep his promise one day.

Lewis considers this a key moment in his life. "Meeting Ron Dennis, making that promise, it fueled my dreams," Lewis reflected. "It made me believe I could make it to Formula One. It made me believe I was born to race."

As Lewis got older, his dreams of racing got bigger. He moved from karting to junior racing categories, each level a new challenge. The journey was tough, especially financially. Racing is expensive and Lewis's dad, Anthony, worked many jobs to afford it. Sometimes, they didn't know if they could pay for the next race. But Anthony always encouraged Lewis to keep racing, promising they'd find a way. "Looking back, I see how much my dad sacrificed for my dream," Lewis says. "I wasn't just racing for me, but for my dad too."

Besides money issues, Lewis also had to deal with tough competition and pressure. He was often the youngest and least experienced racer, but he used these challenges as motivation. Every setback made him more determined. Each loss taught him something new, and every win brought him closer to his dream. "There were times when I felt like I wasn't good enough, or the pressure was too much," Lewis admits. "But every time I raced, I felt I belonged. I knew I had to keep going."

One such moment was during the 2003 Formula Renault UK Championship. The competition was fierce, the stakes high. Halfway through the season, 18-year-old Lewis was lagging behind. Lewis persevered and ended up winning the Championship, marking a significant milestone in his racing career.

The season's penultimate race at Donington Park was one that truly encapsulated Lewis's determination and drive. With the Championship in sight, yet still out of grasp, the race was set to be a thriller. The track was slick from earlier rain, and the air was charged with tension.

Among the competitors were his fiercest rivals, Alex Lloyd and Jamie Green. Alex, known for his aggressive driving style, was leading the points table, while Jamie's technical finesse had won him many fans. Lewis knew he had to give everything to beat them.

"You've got this, Lewis," his coach whispered in his ear before the race. "Remember what we worked on. Stay focused and drive your race."

The roar of the engines filled the air as the lights went out. Lewis's heart pounded in his chest. He fought for position, skilfully navigating the wet track and avoiding collisions. Midway through the race, he found himself behind Alex, struggling to find a way past.

It was then that he recalled his mentor's words: "In racing, as in life, you must seize the moment." Lewis saw an opening on the inside of the notorious hairpin turn, and with a daring move, he overtook Alex.

But the race was far from over. Jamie was closing in, and the final laps were a nail-biting duel. In the end, Lewis's skill and determination prevailed, and he crossed the finish line first.

In 2007, when Lewis was 22, he received a life-changing call. It was McLaren; they wanted him to race for them.

"When I got the call, I was in disbelief," Lewis says. "I kept thinking about when I was ten and told Ron Dennis I would race for him. Now, it was happening. My dream was coming true."

Joining McLaren meant competing with the best in the world. The pressure was high, but Lewis was ready.

His rookie year was a mix of challenges and opportunities. One big challenge was his relationship with teammate Fernando Alonso, a double world champion initially seen as McLaren's lead driver. However, Lewis's excellent performance that first season blurred these lines, leading to a rivalry that added another tricky layer to his rookie year.

In his first year in Formula One, Lewis focused on learning the sport at a deeper level and proving to himself and the world that he deserved to be there. Despite the challenges, he finished the season strongly, securing third place in the World Championship and winning multiple races. This success solidified his position as a formidable force and a future champion.

The year 2008 was particularly exciting for Lewis as he aimed for the World Championship. The season was filled with ups and downs, victories and setbacks, testing his skills, strategic thinking, and mental fortitude in every moment.

This resilience was showcased in the season's final race in Brazil. In this dramatic, rain-soaked event, the Championship was uncertain until the last corner of the last lap. Lewis was trailing, but he didn't give up. In a thrilling moment, he overtook Timo Glock from Toyota in the final seconds, securing fifth place and becoming the World Champion.

"The last lap in Brazil was the longest lap of my life," Lewis remembers. "The rain, the tension, the stakes - it was all too high. But I knew I had to keep my cool, I had to push through. And when I crossed the finish line, when I realized I was the World Champion, it was an indescribable feeling."

At 23 years and 300 days old, Lewis became the youngest-ever World Champion in Formula One history. His victory was more than just a personal triumph; it was a historic moment.

"Winning the World Championship was a dream come true," Lewis says. "But it was also a reminder - a reminder to never stop dreaming, to never stop fighting, no matter how tough the journey gets."

Following his triumph in 2008, Lewis encountered some of the most challenging years of his career. From 2009 to 2012, despite his full dedication, he failed to clinch the Championship. An underperforming car and unexpected race outcomes kept victory elusive.

"Those years were tough," Lewis concedes. "I was giving my all, but the pieces weren't falling into place. It was frustrating, and there were moments of self-doubt. However, those setbacks taught me a lot."

Instead of being deterred, Lewis used these challenges to propel himself forward. He intensified his training, put in extra effort, and spent hours analyzing his races to identify areas of improvement. He was certain that the situation would eventually improve, and he needed to be patient and persistent.

"There's a quote I love - 'Success is not final, failure is not fatal: It is the courage to continue that counts,'" shares Lewis, referring to the famous words of Winston Churchill."

I often reminded myself of that. I knew I had the talent, passion, and drive. I just needed to keep going."

During this time, Lewis also made a pivotal decision: to leave McLaren, the team he'd been with since his debut, and join Mercedes. Many deemed this a risky move, but Lewis felt it was the right step for him.

"Leaving McLaren was one of the hardest decisions I've ever made," Lewis says. "But I felt it was the right thing to do. I needed a fresh start, a new challenge. And joining Mercedes, it felt like the right fit."

In 2013, a new chapter in Hamilton's racing story began. He had joined the Silver Arrows, the Mercedes Formula One team, marking a significant shift in his career. The move was met with curiosity and skepticism. Some questioned whether leaving McLaren, a team synonymous with his early successes, was the right decision. But Lewis felt that it was time for a fresh challenge.

At Mercedes, Lewis Hamilton was paired with Nico Rosberg, a former friend and karting teammate. Their intense rivalry for the World Championship strained their relationship but also pushed Lewis to achieve remarkable success, including multiple world titles.

"Mercedes is more than just a team, it's a family," Lewis says. "We worked together, we celebrated together, and we faced challenges together. It was an incredible journey, one that I'm immensely proud to be a part of."

As Hamilton's journey with Mercedes unfolded, an exceptional phenomenon was taking place. Each race, each season, brought with it new records shattered, new heights reached. He equaled and then surpassed the great Michael Schumacher's record of 91 Grand Prix wins, a feat many thought was unbeatable. Then, he matched and went beyond Schumacher's seven World Championships, standing atop the Formula One world like none other before him.

"Behind every win, every record, there's an immense amount of hard work," says Lewis. "It's the time spent in the gym, the countless laps around the track, the endless hours working with the team. It's a continuous journey of learning, improving, and pushing the boundaries."

One of the most unforgettable races in Lewis Hamilton's time with Mercedes, a race that really showed his toughness and never-give-up attitude, was the 2020 British Grand Prix.

It was a beautiful day at the famous Silverstone Circuit. Now 35 and a top driver with Mercedes, Lewis was ready. The race was about to start, the crowd was excited, and everyone was watching closely.

As the race went on, Lewis was doing great, leading the pack with the finish line in sight. But then, trouble hit on the very last lap. His front-left tyre burst, shooting out sparks as his car wobbled, threatening to spin off the track.

But Lewis didn't panic. He remembered his dad's words, "Still I rise," and it gave him the strength to keep going. He was not going to give up. Not now.

With a determined look, he kept control of the shaky car, guiding it around the circuit. Every turn was tough as he fought to keep the struggling Mercedes on track. Meanwhile, Max Verstappen, a strong competitor, was getting closer, seeing a chance in Lewis's problem. But Lewis didn't back down.

With amazing grit, he crossed the finish line, driving his sparking Mercedes on a busted tyre. The crowd cheered loudly, amazed at what Lewis had done that day - it was a moment that showed he's one of the best in the sport.

Lewis Hamilton's story is one of determination and inspiration, from his humble beginnings in Stevenage to becoming a record-breaking racer and advocate for change. His legacy continues to inspire the next generation of racers to dream big and race with heart.

LEBRON JAMES
"KING JAMES"

The deafening roar of the crowd echoed through the grand Quicken Loans Arena in Cleveland, Ohio. The clock was ticking down in the 2016 NBA Finals, and the tension in the air was so thick you could feel it. LeBron James, then 31 years old, wiped the sweat from his brow, bouncing the ball rhythmically on the gleaming wooden court. "This was it," LeBron thought, "The moment to change everything."

Opposite LeBron and his Cleveland Cavaliers stood the Golden State Warriors, a formidable team famous for their agility and sharp-shooting abilities. But LeBron was not scared. No, he was ready. He looked at his teammates, each of them mirroring his determination, "One more shot. We can do this," he reminded them.

LeBron felt the weight of the entire city on his shoulders. With less than two minutes left, the game was tied. With less than two minutes left, the game was tied. The Warriors had possession of the ball. As they advanced, one of the Warriors' players took a shot. The crowd went silent. In that split second, LeBron's instinct kicked in. He soared through the air like a superhero, extending his arm, and performed 'The Block,' one of the most legendary moves in basketball history. He denied the Warriors a lead, and the crowd erupted in euphoric cheers.

In the final minutes, the Cavaliers secured their victory, and the joyous roar of the crowd was deafening. LeBron fell to his knees, his eyes welling up. He had done it. They had done it. For the first time in over fifty years, Cleveland had won a major sports championship.

He later recalled in an interview, "In those final seconds, my entire life flashed before my eyes. I saw my mom, my kids, Akron...Everything I had gone through was for this moment. I knew then, that no matter where life took me, I'd always fight for my dreams just like I fought for that ball."

On December 30th, 1984, a future star was born in Akron, Ohio. LeBron Raymone James was welcomed into the world by his single mother, Gloria James. Gloria had to face the challenges of parenthood alone, as LeBron's father, an ex-convict, was absent.

LeBron's early life was tough, as he and his mother constantly moved between small apartments. Despite the difficulties, Gloria's love and dedication made LeBron feel cherished. "She was my mother, my father, my everything. She's the reason I have been able to achieve anything," LeBron often reflected.

From the start, LeBron showed great energy and ambition. His first basketball court was his living room, where he copied the moves of players he saw on TV. He soon found a sanctuary in a nearby park where he could run faster than most of the older kids.

LeBron's love for basketball started to flourish at the age of five when a local coach, Bruce Kelker, gifted him a mini basketball hoop. That ignited a passion in LeBron that grew over the years. "The day I received that hoop, my life changed," LeBron once said.

By nine, LeBron was playing organized basketball. He was taller, faster, and stronger than his peers. But it wasn't just his physical skills that made him stand out—it was his resilience and drive. His leadership qualities were evident, always motivating and supporting his teammates.

In the early 1990s, young LeBron and his mother, Gloria, faced the world together. Without a steady income, they often had to move between cramped apartments in Akron, Ohio. Some nights, dinner was no more than a bowl of Cheerios cereal, but they always shared it with a smile.

Despite their circumstances, Gloria made sure that LeBron never missed a day of school or basketball practice. She was a cheerleader, mentor, and most importantly, his number one fan.

LeBron saw how his mother juggled multiple jobs, yet she always found the time to help him with his homework or cheer him up when he was feeling low. "She made me believe that I could do anything," LeBron recalled, "Even when we had nothing, she made me feel like we had everything."

The relationship between LeBron and his mother, Gloria, deepened when she made the difficult decision to send him to live with Frank Walker, his Pee Wee football coach, for a more stable environment. LeBron was only nine, but he understood his mother's sacrifice, promising to make her proud.

In his new home, LeBron experienced a regular lifestyle with his own room, consistent meals, and a more structured routine. This stability helped him concentrate on his education and basketball.

Gloria, though living separately, remained an integral part of LeBron's life. She attended all his games and was his most enthusiastic supporter. LeBron could always pick out her voice from the crowd, and it motivated him when he needed it the most. LeBron often mentioned, "Every day I wake up, I aim to make my mom proud. She's my hero."

In 1995, LeBron, a lean, tall eleven-year-old boy, joined St. Vincent-St. Mary High School in Akron, Ohio. There, he met Coach Dru Joyce who recognized LeBron's raw talent and began nurturing it.

Coach Joyce saw a unique spark in LeBron. He was not just gifted but also possessed an incredible work ethic and determination. Under Coach Joyce's guidance, LeBron's skills began to flourish. He was not only becoming a better player but also a better teammate. "Basketball isn't just about the score," LeBron once said, "It's about teamwork, about always being there for your teammates." This lesson from Coach Joyce stayed with him for life.

Life at St. Vincent wasn't just about basketball. LeBron, the star player, was also LeBron, the diligent student. His mother's words, "Education is your ticket to life," echoed in his mind, pushing him to balance his academics with his love for the sport.

In the year 2000, a 15-year-old LeBron was making waves in the world of high school basketball. As the star player of his team, the 'Fighting Irish,' he led them to a Division III state title win. His impressive performances were pulling him closer to his dream of playing in the NBA. Despite the increasing attention he was receiving, LeBron remained focused and humble. He often said, "All the attention is great, but it doesn't mean anything if I don't stay focused on my game."

By the time he graduated high school in 2002, LeBron was a well-known name in basketball. His next step was the NBA, a goal he had been working towards for years. But even as he stood on the brink of this exciting new chapter, he remembered where he came from - the humble beginnings, his mother's sacrifices, his coach's belief in him, and the important life lessons he learned during his time at St. Vincent-St. Mary High School.

In 2002, LeBron James was finishing high school and hoping to join the NBA. He was very popular and many people thought he was going to be a big basketball star. One day, he had a game against another good player named Lenny Cooke. This was an important game because it could help LeBron get into the NBA.

In a head-to-head showdown, LeBron outscored Cooke and led his team to victory. This win not only solidified LeBron's status as a future star but also taught him a valuable lesson about handling pressure.

Simultaneously, LeBron was wrestling with a big decision: to go to college or to go directly into the NBA. Many advised him to get a college education first, but LeBron knew his heart was set on the NBA.

The decision weighed heavily on him. In an interview, LeBron said, "I remember many nights, looking at the ceiling, wondering if I'm making the right choice." But in the end, LeBron followed his gut, deciding to forgo college and declaring for the 2003 NBA draft.

In 2003, 18-year-old LeBron James, already towering at 6'9" tall, was selected as the first overall pick by the Cleveland Cavaliers. Jim Paxson, the General Manager at the time, saw immense potential in LeBron and was instrumental in choosing him for the team. His first season was filled with excitement, pressure, and learning. In his debut game against the Sacramento Kings, he showed his potential by scoring an impressive 25 points. LeBron learned to cope with the intense scrutiny and pressure, saying, "When I step onto the court, I put all the noise aside. It's just me, my team, and the ball. That's all that matters."

However, adapting to the NBA wasn't only about basketball. LeBron also had to manage the challenges of fame, financial responsibility, and personal growth, saying, "Basketball was the easy part. The hard part was growing up in the public eye." Despite these obstacles, LeBron excelled. He averaged 20.9 points, 5.5 rebounds, and 5.9 assists per game in his first season, winning the Rookie of the Year title. But more importantly, this season was a testament to LeBron's resilience and personal growth at a very young age.

In 2010, seven years into his NBA career, LeBron faced another crossroads. He was a superstar, but his team, the Cleveland Cavaliers, had not secured a championship title. LeBron was hungry for more.

The decision came like a summer storm, unexpected and powerful. "I'm taking my talents to South Beach," LeBron announced on a live television broadcast. The choice to move to the Miami Heat was met with a mix of shock, anger, and excitement. The city of Cleveland felt betrayed, but for LeBron, it was a chance to grow and, hopefully, win.

LeBron's transition to Miami was challenging. "It was like I was the new kid at school and everyone was watching me," he confessed. Along with a new team came new teammates, among them, Chris Bosh and Dwyane Wade. They formed the 'Big Three,' a dynamic trio that would take the Miami Heat to new heights.

LeBron's first season in Miami was a trial by fire. Despite their best efforts, the Heat fell short in the NBA Finals. "That loss was tough," LeBron admitted, "But it was also a wake-up call. I realized I had to work harder, be better."

And all of the hard work paid off, taking them to the final.

It was 2012 NBA Finals and the Miami Heat faced off against the Oklahoma City Thunder, led by the talented Kevin Durant. The pressure was immense; the spotlight was on LeBron, and the world was watching.

Game 2 of the series had everyone on the edge of their seats. Miami was trailing by one point with just 15 seconds left on the clock. The stadium was a sea of Thunder blue, but the Heat fans could be heard chanting LeBron's name, faith in their eyes.

LeBron took a deep breath, wiped the sweat from his brow, and looked to his coach. The play was set, the team was ready. LeBron caught the ball, dribbled past multiple defenders in a blurred flurry, and found himself facing his arch rival, Durant. They exchanged a glance, a momentary recognition of each other's skill and determination.

Time seemed to slow as LeBron made his move. With an intelligent and powerful leap, he shot the ball, and the crowd held its breath. The ball swished through the net just as the buzzer sounded. Victory! The Miami Heat won the game and eventually went on to win the series.

The celebrations were ecstatic, but LeBron knew that the battle was not over. The next year, facing Tim Duncan and the San Antonio Spurs, he would have to dig even deeper, push even harder. But the 2013 Finals was a story of triumph as well, as LeBron led the Heat to a second consecutive championship.

Those years in Miami were filled with sweat, tears, and glory. LeBron had proved that he could conquer anything on the court, even himself. He had risen above rivalries, silenced doubters, and brought home the coveted trophy, not once but twice.

"If I can conquer my doubts, I can conquer anything on the court." He said during an interview after the wins.

LeBron's return to Cleveland in 2014 was a moment that tugged at the heartstrings of fans everywhere. The prodigal son was coming home, and the air was thick with hope. Years had passed since he left, but his connection to his hometown remained as strong as ever. Now, he was back, wearing the colors of the Cleveland Cavaliers once again, the team where it all began.

He was ready to embrace the challenge, ready to fight for his home team, ready to bring glory to Cleveland. His eyes, filled with passion and resolve, said it all: He was home, and he was here to win.

The prodigal son had returned, but would he be able to bring glory to his home team?

"Before anyone ever cared where I would play basketball, I was a kid from Northeast Ohio. It's where I learnt basketball. It's where I trained. It's where I bled,"

The move was about more than basketball – it was about coming home.

As he donned his familiar Cavaliers jersey, LeBron felt the weight of expectations. He was no longer the young player from Akron with great potential; he was a seasoned champion, carrying the hopes of an entire city on his shoulders.

Despite their best efforts, the Cavaliers lost to the Golden State Warriors in the 2015 NBA Finals. LeBron, however, was not deterred. He was bent on winning, not just for himself, but for his home. "I didn't come back to Cleveland to lose," he declared.

The following season was a testament to LeBron's determination and hard work. His leadership on and off the court was instrumental in taking the Cavaliers to the NBA Finals again in 2016. This time, they were facing the same team that had defeated them a year ago - the Golden State Warriors.

The Cavaliers were down 3-1 in the series. LeBron, however, was not ready to give up. He rallied his team, reminding them of what they were playing for - their city, their pride, and their legacy.

In Game 7 of the 2016 NBA Finals, with less than two minutes left, LeBron made an iconic block against Andre Iguodala of the Warriors. This pivotal moment became known as "The Block," symbolizing LeBron's relentless determination and resilience.

The Cleveland Cavaliers won the game and the championship - their first in franchise history. LeBron, with tears streaming down his face, declared, "Cleveland, this is for you!" This victory was more than just a title; it was the fulfillment of a promise he had made to his home.

In 2018, LeBron James, hungry to prove himself further, chose the challenge of joining the Los Angeles Lakers, a franchise rich in history and star players. He saw in the Lakers a chance to walk alongside legends like Kobe Bryant.

"The purple and gold, it's more than just a uniform. It's a symbol of excellence," LeBron declared at his introductory press conference.

When LeBron moved to Los Angeles, he had the big task of reviving a team that had been struggling.

In 2020, during the global pandemic, LeBron led the Lakers to their 17th NBA Championship. This win wasn't just about another trophy; it was about continuing the legacy of the Lakers. "We're not just playing for ourselves, we're playing for all the greats who wore the purple and gold before us," LeBron said after the victory.

LeBron took a step beyond the basketball court that would define his legacy in an entirely different way. He opened the doors to the 'I PROMISE' school in his hometown of Akron, Ohio, a beacon of hope for children in need.

His eyes filled with compassion, LeBron said, "I know what these kids are going through. I want to give them the tools to succeed."

The school was more than just bricks and mortar; it was a promise, a commitment. Free school, uniforms, food, and the unwavering support to guide them into college. And it didn't stop there. LeBron's partnership with the University of Akron provided scholarships, forging a path where dreams could become realities.

In LeBron James, the world found not just a basketball legend, but a hero who taught us to keep trying, even when the odds are stacked against us. A role model who showed us that hard work and self-belief can conquer the highest mountains. As the story of LeBron's life unfolds, we are reminded that greatness is not only measured by what we achieve but by what we give back. In his unbreakable promise to those children, LeBron found his true victory, a victory of the heart, leaving a legacy that will continue to inspire for generations to come.

On a sunny afternoon of September 4, 1993, a hush descended over Yankee Stadium in New York in a game between the Cleveland Indians and the Yankees. Thousands of eyes watched as Jim Abbott, a southpaw with just one hand, walked onto the field. The hushed whispers of the crowd echoed, "Can he do it? Can he pitch a no-hitter?"

Abbott didn't let the tension in the air bother him. With a deep breath, he focused on the catcher's mitt, blocking out the sea of people around him.

The game progressed, and the whispers turned into loud cheers as Abbott skillfully struck out batter after batter. The ninth inning arrived. The anticipation was tangible. "Three more outs," someone shouted. "Just three more, Abbott!" This was it - the moment that could carve his name in history.

His heart pounded in his chest, but he didn't let it show. He focused on his strength, remembering all the adversities he'd faced and overcome in his journey to this moment. Drawing on his reservoir of mental toughness, he tossed the final pitch, holding his breath as the batter swung - and missed! A deafening roar erupted from the crowd. Jim Abbott, the one-handed pitcher, had just thrown a no-hitter, a feat many with two hands could only dream of.

As his teammates rushed to celebrate, Abbott felt a surge of triumph, a testament to his tenacity, hard work, and unfaltering belief. He had thrown a no-hitter, establishing his name into the journals of baseball history. This was the climax of his story, but how did he get there? For that, we must go back to the beginning.

It all started in Flint, Michigan, in the year 1967. In a small house filled with love, a baby boy was born. His name was Jim Abbott. But, there was something different about Jim – he was born without a right hand. From day one, Jim was different. But in the eyes of his parents, Mike and Kathy Abbott, Jim was not different, but special.

Mike and Kathy were the type of parents who believed in possibilities rather than limitations. They refused to treat Jim any differently from other kids. "Life is not about what you don't have, but what you do with what you have," Mike would often tell Jim.

During his early years, they encouraged him to play, explore, and be just like any other child. "Go on, Jim, you can do it!" Kathy would encourage, her eyes sparkling with warmth and belief, every time Jim tried something new.

They taught him to tie his shoes, to write, and even to catch a baseball with one hand. They cheered him on every step of the way, celebrating his small victories, their faith in him unshakeable.

When things got tough, they were there, whispering words of encouragement, nurturing the seeds of resilience in their son.

As Jim grew, he was armed with his parents' wisdom and their unwavering belief in him. He carried his father's words like a secret weapon, "Jim, your strength lies in your will, not in your hand."

At an early age, Jim discovered a world where he truly felt at home: the world of sports. He was an active child, always out playing with his friends. Whether it was basketball, football, or baseball, Jim loved it all. But there was something special about baseball, a charm that had Jim completely hooked.

As Jim grew, so did his passion for baseball. He was a natural athlete, but his one-handedness presented a unique challenge. But where most saw a challenge, Jim saw an opportunity. He began to work on a technique where he would rest his glove on the stump of his right arm. After catching the ball, he'd quickly slip his left hand into the glove, securing the ball, then pull it out to throw. It was a complicated maneuver, but Jim practiced until it became second nature.

The neighborhood games were full of laughter, cheers, and friendly rivalry. But they were also sprinkled with doubts and skepticism. Not everyone believed a one-handed boy could play baseball. "Are you sure you can do this, Jim?" they'd ask, their eyes reflecting doubt. But Jim, filled with determination, would just smile and say, "Just watch me!"

And he showed them, time and again, that he could. He fielded, he batted, he threw, he scored. With each game, he proved that he was not just ordinary, but extraordinary. He wasn't merely playing; he was excelling. And with each win, the doubts and skepticism began to fade, replaced by respect and admiration.

While baseball remained his first love, Jim didn't shy away from exploring other sports. He was as much at home on the football field as he was on the baseball diamond. As the quarterback of the school football team, he surprised many with his precise passes and quick decision-making. His one hand didn't hold him back; if anything, it fueled him to work harder, train longer, and play smarter.

However, his road wasn't always smooth. There were times when he faced skeptics, those who questioned if a one-handed boy could compete at such a high level. But every doubtful gaze, every murmur of uncertainty, only strengthened Jim's spirit. He would meet their skepticism with a steely determination and a confident smile. "Doubt me, and I'll prove you wrong," he'd say, his eyes gleaming with resolve.

Jim's relentless grit shone on the baseball field, where he was nothing short of a star. His pitches were fast and accurate, his fielding smooth and effortless. He led his team to many victories, earning the respect and admiration of his teammates, coaches, and even his critics.

In the process, he became more than just an athlete. He became an inspiration, a beacon of resilience, showing everyone that limitations only exist if you let them. His high school triumphs were just a glimpse of the heights he would eventually reach.

From Flint Central High School, Jim's journey took him to the University of Michigan, where he was welcomed into the Wolverines baseball team. College baseball was a step up, the stakes were higher, and the competition was tougher. But Jim didn't flinch. He was ready to take on the challenge.

At Michigan, Jim evolved as a player. His pitching got sharper, his confidence grew, and his name began to resonate in college baseball circles. He was not just a one-handed baseball player anymore. He became a formidable southpaw. He was a leader, the heart of the team, his spirit of determination infectious.

Yet it wasn't all about glory and accolades. There were defeats, moments of self-doubt, and criticism. But each setback was a lesson, each failure a stepping stone.

But the pinnacle of his early career came in the summer of 1988. Jim was chosen to represent Team USA in the Olympics in Seoul. To stand on the Olympic field was an honor, a dream that he'd harbored since he first fell in love with the game.

Donning the USA jersey, Jim showed the world what he was made of. Throughout the tournament, Abbott lived up to this trust. His pitching skills shone brilliantly, contributing significantly to his team's progress towards victory. Each strike he threw, each batter he retired, brought Team USA closer to the gold. The culmination of this journey came when he stood on the victory podium, a gold medal hanging around his neck. The Star-Spangled Banner - the national anthem of the United States - rang out in the stadium, honoring the victorious team and, specifically, Jim's incredible performance.

For Abbott, this moment was not just a personal victory but a testament to his determination, talent, and resilience in the face of all odds. His Olympic success, particularly as a one-handed pitcher, made this achievement all the more remarkable and inspiring.

The year 1989 marked a monumental leap in Jim's journey. Drafted by the California Angels, he was ready to make his mark in the Major Leagues.

Jim vividly remembered the first day he set foot onto the Major League field. The stadium was colossal, the crowd deafening, and the air pulsated with excitement. Jim looked at his glove, then at the sprawling field, and said to himself, "This is it, Jim. It's your time to shine."

And shine, he did! His rookie season was nothing short of sensational. With every game, he showed his prowess, his skill, and his love for the game. The young lad from Flint, Michigan, was now a force to be reckoned with in the world's toughest baseball league.

The highlight of his debut season was his game against the mighty Toronto Blue Jays. Pitching against some of the best hitters in the game, Jim showed remarkable composure. His fastballs zipped across the field, leaving the opposition clueless. After the game, he cheerfully remarked to his teammate, "I guess the Blue Jays' wings weren't fast enough for my pitches!"

Jim finished his rookie season with an impressive 12-12 record, a remarkable achievement for a newcomer. His impressive performance earned him the title of California Angels' Rookie of the Year. His entry into the Major Leagues was like a comet streaking across the sky - bright, spectacular, and unforgettable.

The world of Major League Baseball was intense. Jim quickly learned that every game was a battle, every opponent a challenge. And with challenges, came rivalries.

One of Jim's most formidable rivals was the quick and powerful Roger Clemens. Known for his blistering fastballs, Clemens was a titan in the world of baseball, a pitcher par excellence. Every time Jim stepped onto the field against Clemens, he knew he was in for a duel. But Jim never backed down. He stood firm, reminding himself before every pitch, "I'm not here to fear. I'm here to fight!"

There was a game against the Boston Red Sox that particularly tested Jim's mettle. It was a chilly evening, the crowd was roaring, and Clemens was on fire. But Jim held his own, matching Clemens pitch for pitch. The game went into extra innings, a nerve-wracking tug of war. At one point, in the heat of the moment, Jim muttered to himself, "This isn't just a game. It's a battle of wills."

Despite the pressure, Jim showed remarkable composure. He might have been a young player, but his tenacity was that of a seasoned pro.

Though the Angels lost the game, Jim walked off the field with his head held high, knowing he'd given his all.

Facing challenges and dealing with professional pressures was a part of Jim's journey in the Major Leagues. There were times when he faltered, moments when he tasted defeat. But he never let those moments define him. Instead, he used them as stepping stones, climbing the professional ladder with grit, grace, and resilience.

His journey in the Major Leagues was far from over; there were many more games to play, many more battles to win.

Even heroes have their kryptonite. For Jim, the year 1992 proved to be his. That year, he experienced his most challenging season. His performance dipped, the wins were fewer, and whispers of doubt started to circle.

One game against the Detroit Tigers was particularly disheartening. As the runs against him stacked up, he felt his confidence waver. Walking off the field that day, he felt a heavy weight on his shoulders. He confided in his teammate, "It's like I've forgotten how to pitch."

The struggles didn't end there. Soon, he was traded to the New York Yankees. Leaving the Angels was a difficult moment for Jim. California had become his home, the Angels his family. But the world of professional sports was unpredictable, and Jim knew he had to adapt.

Instead of letting this bring him down, Jim took it as a fresh start. The Yankees had a legacy of champions, and Jim was determined to be a part of that legacy. As he put on the pinstriped jersey for the first time, he said, "It's not about where you play; it's about how you play."

Jim used his struggles as fuel, working tirelessly to improve his game. He spent hours on the field, perfecting his pitches, and honing his skills. He faced his disappointments head-on, learning from his mistakes and growing stronger with every setback.

Jim's resilience shone through his dark times. He believed in his ability to turn things around, to rise from the ashes. "Tough times never last, but tough people do," he would say, an echo of his undying spirit.

As the summer of 1993 drew to a close, Jim was entering a new chapter in his career with the Yankees. After a year of battles and struggles, he felt more prepared, more focused. He had tasted defeat, weathered the storm, and now it was time to shine. Little did he know, an unforgettable day was on the horizon.

The stage was set on September 4, 1993. The Yankees were up against the Cleveland Indians at Yankee Stadium. As Jim warmed up, he could feel the electric anticipation of the crowd. But amidst the excitement, Jim was calm. He had a premonition. As he once confessed, "Before the game started, I felt unusually calm. It felt different, special even."

The first innings went smoothly. Jim's pitches were on point, his focus unwavering. He kept the Indians at bay. One after the other, the batters returned to the dugout, their bats silent against Jim's throws.

With each passing inning, the crowd grew quieter, holding their breath as they realized what was unfolding before their eyes. By the seventh inning, everyone knew something special was happening. Jim, however, remained unfazed, focusing on his pitches, blocking out the noise.

Finally, it was the bottom of the ninth. The stadium was silent, every eye fixed on Jim. He took a deep breath, stared down at the batter, and hurled his pitch. A swing and a miss. The crowd erupted. Jim Abbott, the pitcher with one hand, had just thrown a no-hitter, a feat achieved by only a few in the history of Major League Baseball.

In that moment of sheer elation, Jim stood on the mound, absorbing the cheers, the applause, the realization of what he had achieved. With a smile on his face, he uttered, "Today, I didn't just pitch a game, I lived a dream."

That day, Jim Abbott didn't just throw a no-hitter. He showcased an extraordinary display of courage, mental toughness, and exceptional skill. It was a testament to his perseverance, a reminder to every young dreamer that no obstacle is too big to overcome. It was, without a doubt, the shining moment of his career.

With the close of the 1999 season, Jim Abbott retired from professional baseball. The diamond that had been his stage for so long, now awaited new heroes. But for Jim, a new inning was about to begin - a journey off the field.

He took off on a career as a motivational speaker, using his unique story to inspire millions around the globe. Whether it was a room full of eager students or an auditorium packed with executives, Jim's message resonated. "You're not defined by your circumstances, but by your actions," he often said, reflecting on his life journey.

In the world of baseball, he will forever be remembered as the one-handed pitcher who threw a no-hitter. But his legacy goes beyond that.

Jim Abbott's story serves as a beacon of hope, inspiring countless people to overcome their challenges and chase their dreams, no matter how distant they may seem.

He once said, "Life is a team sport, and we all have the ability to lift those around us." And that's what he did. With every pitch, every struggle, every triumph, Jim lifted the spirits of those who watched him, showing us that heroes are not defined by their challenges, but by their courage to overcome them.

As our tale ends, the lessons it leaves behind resonate – the power of perseverance, the strength of resilience, and the courage to chase your dreams, no matter the odds. Because at the heart of it all, Jim Abbott's story is not just about baseball. It's about the game of life. And in that game, we can all be champions, regardless of out circumstances.

SIMONE BILES
"$IMONEY"

Tokyo, a city bustling with bright lights and excitement, was holding its breath. Inside the grand Olympic Stadium, eyes were glued to Simone Biles. At 24 years old in 2021, Simone was the shining star of gymnastics, and everyone was eagerly waiting for her to dazzle them with her incredible moves. But then, something unexpected happened: Simone decided not to compete. This decision was even bigger and more astonishing than any gymnastics move she had ever made.

"Sometimes, we have to choose between what others want and what we want," she later explained. Her choice was brave and showed her remarkable strength and spirit. But this wasn't a decision made on a whim. It was a big moment that had been years in the making, even before she became an Olympian.

To understand this choice, we go back to her beginnings in Texas. Here, Simone Biles, a young girl, started her journey to become one of the greatest female gymnasts to ever live.

Back in 1997, when Simone was only three years old, a big change happened. She and her little sister, Adria, were living in Columbus, Ohio. Their mother was having a tough time and couldn't take care of them. That's when their grandparents, Nellie and Ron Biles, stepped in. They decided to adopt Simone and Adria. From that day on, Nellie and Ron became their new mom and dad.

Simone feels very thankful for her grandparents. She once said, "They've given us a chance at life." The early days were hard, but Simone, Adria, Nellie, and Ron faced it all together. They became a strong family, and this helped Simone grow into a brave person.

One day, the family went on a trip to a place called Bannon's Gymnastix, a local gymnastics center. They thought it would be a fun way to spend the day. But for Simone, it became much more than that. She saw gymnasts flipping and twirling in the air. She thought it was amazing! Before anyone could stop her, Simone ran and jumped into a foam pit. She did her own somersaults and had lots of fun. Her mom and dad saw this and smiled. They saw that Simone had a special talent. Simone was just like any other kid. She loved to play, but gymnastics was something special for her. She loved the feeling of flying in the air, turning, and flipping.

One day, a coach at the gym noticed Simone. The coach was amazed by Simone's talent. She saw Simone doing flips and turns as if she was born to do it. She said, "Simone, you are built for this!"

Hearing those words, Simone felt happy and excited. But she also knew that gymnastics was a tough sport. She had to train hard. It meant long hours in the gym, practicing again and again until she got it just right.

While she showed an undeniable talent at just six years old, she actually had quite a late start for formal training at the age of 10, when compared to other gymnasts. Despite this late start, Bannon's Gymnastix, the same place where she first saw people flipping and twirling, became the launching pad for her love of gymnastics.

Besides gymnastics, Simone also had school to take care of. It wasn't easy balancing schoolwork with training. But Simone was determined. She made a promise to herself to do her best in both school and gymnastics. With a sparkle in her eyes and a dream in her heart, Simone took her first steps into the big world of gymnastics.

The world of gymnastics is full of jumps, flips, and, most importantly, hard work. And Simone was ready for it all. She was training really hard, sometimes even until her muscles ached. But Simone loved every minute of it. She once said, "Hard days are the best because that's when champions are made!"

The year was 2009, and the stage was set for her first significant competition: the American Classic in Huntsville, Texas.

As the day approached, Simone's excitement mixed with nerves. This was a different world, filled with talented competitors, some of whom were older and more experienced. Names like Rebecca Bross and Bridget Sloan, gymnasts she had looked up to, were now her competitors. She would be participating in the all-around event, showcasing her skills on the vault, uneven bars, balance beam, and floor.

Simone, only 12 years old at the time, stepped onto the mat. The arena was filled with the roar of the crowd, the flash of cameras, and the watchful eyes of judges. She took a deep breath and began her routine on the vault, her favorite apparatus. Her performance was a blend of strength and elegance, each twist and flip executed with remarkable precision.

As she moved from the vault to the uneven bars, then to the balance beam and finally the floor, the audience was captivated by her extraordinary skills. Her family cheered her on, their pride evident in their smiles.

When the scores were announced, Simone had not only won but had also made a statement to the world of gymnastics.

This was a big moment for Simone. All her hard work was paying off. But she knew this was just the beginning. She had more flips to make, more jumps to take, and more victories to win. As she held her trophy, Simone smiled and thought, "This is just the beginning. I can't wait to see what's next."

After years of training and dreaming, Simone was ready to move up to the senior level of gymnastics in 2013. She was 16, and she was excited. Simone had always wanted to compete against the best, and now she had her chance.

Her first big test as a senior gymnast came at the P&G Championships, held at the XL Center in Hartford, Connecticut, on August 17th 2013. Simone, now 16 years old, felt a storm of emotions as she prepared to step onto the mat. The arena buzzed with anticipation, filled with the noise of a thousand voices and the harsh glare of spotlights.

She started with the vault, executing a breathtaking Cheng (a roundoff half turn onto the board into a front handspring onto the vault, followed by a layout with one and a half twists). Running full speed, she launched into the air, twisting and turning in ways that made the audience gasp. Her body seemed to defy gravity as she soared, her movements a blend of power and grace.

When she landed, she could barely believe it herself. She had nailed it! The crowd erupted in applause. She was no longer just a promising junior; she was now a force to reckon with at the senior level.

Simone then moved on to the uneven bars, where she performed intricate transitions, swinging smoothly between the bars, her body arched and toes pointed.

Her floor routine was the show-stopping finale, a masterful blend of artistry and athleticism. With explosive tumbling passes, including a soaring double layout with a half-twist (known as "The Biles"), she danced and tumbled her way into the hearts of the audience. Her performance was a combination of joy, strength, and fluidity, and she executed every leap and turn with a smile that radiated confidence.

Looking back, Simone often says, "That was the moment I realized I could really do this. I could compete with the best, and I could win." This belief in herself, fueled by her victory at the P&G Championships, carried Simone forward as she vaulted her way into gymnastics history.

The year 2013 was a challenging one for Simone. After her victorious debut at the senior level, she was ready to take on the world at the World Artistic Gymnastics Championships. However, things didn't go as planned. Simone had a fall on the beam, one of her favorite apparatuses. This misstep cost her dearly, and she didn't perform as well as she had hoped.

Disappointment washed over Simone like a wave. She remembered sitting in her hotel room after the competition, replaying the fall over and over in her head. She felt like she had let everyone down – her family, her coaches, but mostly, herself.

It was her coach's words that helped her put things in perspective. "Simone," he said, "everyone falls. It's how you get back up that defines you as an athlete."

Those words stuck with her. She realized that while she couldn't change the past, she could learn from it. Simone decided to turn her setback into a setup for a comeback.

Over the next year, Simone worked harder than ever. She practiced her routines until they were flawless. She worked on her mental toughness, learning to block out distractions and focus on her performance.

When the 2014 World Artistic Gymnastics Championships came around, Simone was ready. This time, when she stepped up to the beam, she was calm and confident. She performed her routine without a hitch and went on to win the competition, becoming a world champion.

Looking back on her journey, Simone often shares, "The only time you should ever look back is to see how far you've come. Every setback is a setup for a comeback."

Simone Biles, the gymnastics dynamo, has always found joy in life's simple pleasures. Like any of us, she relishes the comfort of home-cooked food. After gruelling competitions, she indulges in a beloved tradition, treating herself to a slice of pizza. This celebration, as straightforward as it sounds, signifies much more. "There's nothing like a slice of pizza after a hard day of competition," Simone once admitted, her eyes twinkling with unspoken delight. This small reward, as modest as it seems, mirrors her approach to life — disciplined yet cherishing the delightful moments life offers.

In the summer of 2016, the world's eyes turned to Rio de Janeiro. The Olympics were in full swing, and among the thousands of athletes was a young woman who would leave an indelible mark on gymnastics. Simone Biles, with her infectious smile and unparalleled skill, was set to make history as she represented the USA.

Her performance at the Rio Olympics was a display of gymnastics that the world had never seen before. One by one, she secured gold in the all-around, vault, and floor, her poise and precision leaving spectators and judges in awe. But her crowning glory was yet to come. With her phenomenal routine on the balance beam, Simone secured her fourth gold, becoming the first American gymnast to do so in a single Olympics.

"Every time I stepped onto the mat," she would later say, "I wasn't just doing it for me. I was doing it for everyone who believed in me." The sacrifices her parents had made, from those long drives to the gym to their endless encouragement, now seemed to hold more meaning than ever before.

One could imagine her family's pride as they watched from the stands, their hearts swelling with every flip and twist Simone performed. Their little girl, the same child who had once tumbled and leaped around their living room, was now a beacon of excellence on the world stage. Simone Biles, the golden girl of Rio, had not only reached unprecedented heights but had also forever engraved her name in Olympic history.

Even as Simone Biles soared to incredible heights in the arena, her life was not devoid of hardships.

Her struggle with ADHD, a battle she had fought since childhood, was no secret. In a tweet in 2016, she addressed it candidly: "Having ADHD, and taking medicine for it is nothing to be ashamed of and nothing that I'm afraid to let people know." Simone chose not to hide her diagnosis, but instead, she used her platform to raise awareness and address the stigma surrounding it. She became a beacon of hope for many young people dealing with similar challenges, showing them that it's okay to be different.

But another heavy burden soon came to light. Simone was among the many young women who had been victims of Larry Nassar's abuse, the former USA Gymnastics team doctor. It was a heartbreaking revelation, one that shocked the world and took a severe toll on Simone. However, she refused to be silenced or let her past define her. Instead, she stood strong, confronting the pain and fighting for justice. "We need to know why this was able to take place for so long and to so many of us," she said bravely, her words echoing the sentiment of hundreds of others who had suffered in silence.

Through all the trials and tribulations, Simone continued to inspire millions around the world. She demonstrated that it's not just about the battles you fight in the arena, but also the ones you face in private. The strength and courage she showed in dealing with her personal challenges are a testament to her character, making her story all the more remarkable.

Tokyo 2021 – a city buzzing with the excitement of the Olympics. But for Simone, the city held a different meaning. It was the place where she would make a brave decision that would shock the world but, most importantly, save herself.

After dazzling the world with her performances over the years, Simone had everyone's eyes on her in Tokyo. The anticipation was high. The world was ready to witness another spectacle from the gymnastics queen. But, in an unexpected turn of events, Simone decided to withdraw from the competition. "I have to do what's right for me and focus on my mental health," she announced, taking everyone by surprise.

Suddenly, the air was filled with a mix of confusion, concern, and disbelief. How could the queen of gymnastics step down from her throne? But as Simone explained her reasons, the whispers slowly turned into sounds of understanding and respect. "We have to protect our minds and our bodies and not just go out and do what the world wants us to do," she bravely stated.

She specifically mentioned experiencing a condition known as "the twisties," a disorienting mental block in gymnastics where athletes lose the understanding of their position mid-air. It's a dangerous condition considering the high stakes of the maneuvers performed in the sport.

For those who had followed Simone's journey from the start, her withdrawal wasn't just about Tokyo 2021. It was a testament to the courage she had shown throughout her life, the same courage that had been evident when she was a little girl in Texas, trying to find her place in the world.

Simone's choice in Tokyo became an important lesson in self-care. It reminded us that it's okay to choose ourselves over anything else, even when the world expects otherwise. As Simone has always said, "We cannot be afraid to do what is best for us." It was her way of reinforcing the truth she had been living all her life – the real strength lies in recognizing when you need to step back, heal, and fight another day.

After the 2021 Tokyo Olympics, Simone's life took a new turn. The once little girl from Texas, who dreamed of flying, had become a symbol of strength and resilience. But her story was far from over. With her gymnastics chapter slowly closing, Simone was opening a new one, stepping into a world beyond the mat.

The world had seen Simone the gymnast. Now, it was time to see Simone the advocate, the influencer, and the game-changer. She became a strong voice for athletes, constantly reminding the world about the importance of mental health in sports. "It's okay not to be okay," she would often say, driving home the point that even the greatest champions have their vulnerable moments.

Simone is more than just a champion gymnast. She is a woman of strength, a mental health advocate, and a symbol of resilience. "Life is a journey, and the path may change," Simone said, "but what matters is that you keep moving forward."

And so, Simone continues to move forward, stepping into new roles, breaking new ground, and inspiring millions with her story. Her legacy extends beyond the gymnastics floor, into the hearts of those she has touched, the lives she has changed, and the world that has watched her grow from a young girl with a dream into a woman leaving a lasting legacy.

TOM BRADY
"THE GOAT"

February 5, 2017, millions of people are glued to their television screens, their hearts pounding as the final minutes of Super Bowl LI tick away. The New England Patriots, led by their superstar quarterback, Tom Brady, are locked in an epic struggle with the Atlanta Falcons.

Brady, at 39, is not the youngest player on the field. But his steely blue eyes are alight with determination, and his face is set with a rock-solid resolve. The score stands at 28-28, and the Patriots have one final chance to clinch the game.

As Brady huddles with his team, "Guys, we've worked too hard to let this slip away," he tells his teammates. He sees their heads nod in agreement, their faces reflecting their trust in him. They break the huddle, ready for the most crucial play of their lives.

With the weight of the world on his shoulders, Brady snaps the ball into his hands. He steps back, scanning the field with eagle-eyed precision. He spots an opening and throws the ball with all his might, his sights set on victory.

The stadium falls silent as the ball arcs in the air, then erupts into thunderous cheers as the Patriots score the game-winning touchdown. As Brady lifts his arms in triumph, the crowd chants his name, celebrating the man who turned the tide against impossible odds.

"Brady! Brady! Brady!"

The 'Brady Effect,' as fans like to call it, is this amazing ability to stay cool under pressure, to dig deep when the odds are stacked against him, and to always, always find a way to win. As we journey through his life, you'll see that this 'effect' is not just about football. It's a way of life, it's a mindset, and it all started in a small town called San Mateo...

Born on August 3, 1977, in San Mateo, California, Tom Brady was the fourth child of Tom Brady Sr. and Galynn Patricia Brady. Growing up in a bustling household with three older sisters, he learned the values of humility, perseverance, and hard work.

From a young age, he showed a passion for sports. He excelled in baseball and even caught the attention of pro scouts! But for Tom, baseball was like the opening act to the main event. The game that truly captured his heart was football.

The first taste of football came from watching games with his father. Just imagine, a teeny-tiny 4-year-old Tom Brady at the legendary 1981 NFC Championship Game!

Now, this wasn't any ordinary game. The 49ers were playing against the Dallas Cowboys, and the tension was as thick as the fog that often blankets San Francisco. The crowd was roaring, the players were in top form, and there, amidst all the action, was little Tommy Brady, with his dad.

But instead of cheering or clapping, little Tommy spent the entire game crying! Tears streamed down his rosy cheeks because he was so tiny, and the crowd was so enormous that he couldn't see the field. All he wanted was to watch his heroes in action, but alas, all he could see were the backs of the grown-ups in front of him!

Back then, the two would regularly attend San Francisco 49ers games, where Tom watched Joe Montana, the legendary quarterback, weave his magic on the field. Watching Montana, Tom thought, "I want to do that. I want to be out there, leading the team."

Despite not being the biggest or fastest kid, Tom's love for football was undeniable. His determination and desire to improve compensated for his lack of size. He was often the first to arrive at practice and the last to leave, always honing his skills. His schoolmates nicknamed him the "comeback kid" for his ability to turn games around, and friends would often remark, "Tommy? He always has a football in his hands!"

At Junípero Serra High School, Tom joined the football team, but wasn't initially the first-choice quarterback. Instead of becoming disheartened, Tom was determined to prove his worth. His coach, Tom McKenzie, recognized Tom's relentless spirit and worked closely with him, teaching him the intricacies of football. Tom's abilities grew with every training session, and by his junior year, he became the starting quarterback. His exceptional performances led the team to numerous victories, making him a local hero. Despite his rising popularity, Tom remained humble, acknowledging that hard work, not just talent, contributed to his success.

When Tom arrived at the University of Michigan in 1995, he was a wide-eyed young man brimming with ambition. He joined the Wolverines, one of the top football teams in the country, with one goal in mind: to be the starting quarterback.

But the journey was far from easy. Competition was stiff, and once again, Tom found himself on the bench, biding his time. Among his rivals, one stood out: Drew Henson, a local Michigan star known for his powerful arm and agile moves. The rivalry between Tom and Drew would become one of the defining chapters of Tom's college years.

Imagine how Tom felt, watching from the sidelines while Drew Henson, younger but equally passionate about the game, took the limelight.

It could've been easy to feel defeated, but remember, Tom was no stranger to setbacks. They fueled his determination and resilience.

"There's no elevator to success, you have to take the stairs," his mother used to tell him. Tom held onto this wisdom, putting in extra hours after practice, studying game tapes late into the night.

The turning point came in his junior year when Coach Lloyd Carr gave him a chance to play. Tom seized the opportunity with both hands. His dedication and commitment began to shine through, and his performances on the field improved game after game. The crowd started to chant his name, "Brady! Brady! Brady!"

However, the competition with Henson remained fierce. Henson was not ready to give up the coveted spot without a fight, leading to a quarterback controversy that lasted for the entire 1998 season.

During a crucial match against Iowa in 1998, the tension between Brady and Henson was evident. After Henson was substituted in and threw an intercepted pass that led to an Iowa score, Brady was brought back into the game. With steady determination, Brady led the team to a 12-9 victory, showing his ability to perform under pressure.

Post-game, when asked about the ongoing quarterback controversy, Tom responded, "Football is a team sport, and I'm here to do whatever it takes to help my team win. If that means sharing time with Drew, then that's what I'll do." This demonstrated his selfless approach to the sport.

The year 2000 was a roller coaster ride for Brady. It was the year of the NFL Draft, a momentous event where college football players awaited their fate, hoping to be picked by a professional team. The anticipation was sky-high. Yet, as each pick passed, Brady's name wasn't called.

Brady, the once star quarterback of the Wolverines, watched as 198 other names were called before his. Disappointment is a bitter pill to swallow, especially when your dreams hang in the balance. Yet, it was at this moment that Brady taught us a vital lesson: not all setbacks are roadblocks; some are stepping stones.

With the 199th pick, the New England Patriots chose Tom Brady. Many considered it an unexpected choice, a risk even. But little did they know that this late sixth-round pick would one day become one of the greatest quarterbacks in NFL history.

"When you come to the end of your rope, tie a knot and hang on." Tom once said, a quote that reflected his attitude after the draft. He was down, but not out. The setback lit a fire within him, fueling his motivation to prove that he wasn't just the 199th pick, but a future NFL superstar.

Tom arrived in New England ready to give his all. He didn't have the spotlight. He didn't have the pressure of being a top pick. What he had was a determination as strong as iron and a heart full of passion for the game he loved.

The year 2001 was a defining one in Brady's life. He was 24 years old, a back-up quarterback for the New England Patriots, and yet again on the sidelines, waiting for his chance to prove himself.

The moment came unexpectedly during a game against the New York Jets. Drew Bledsoe, the team's star quarterback, was injured. The crowd held its breath, and then it happened: Brady's number was called.

Can you imagine what was going through his mind? A mix of excitement, fear, and immense pressure. "I remember looking at my teammates in the huddle," Brady later recounted, "knowing they were depending on me to lead them. And all I could think was, 'Don't let them down.'"

Drawing on the mental toughness he had cultivated over the years, Brady stepped onto the field. As he threw his first professional pass, he remembered his parents' words, "Courage isn't the absence of fear, but the triumph over it."

The rest, as they say, is history. Brady led the Patriots to an impressive 11-3 record in the remaining games of the season, proving that he was more than capable of stepping up to the plate. He didn't just fill Bledsoe's shoes; he carved his own path, one that would take him to heights unimaginable for the 199th pick.

February 3, 2002, the Louisiana Superdome buzzing with anticipation, the roar of thousands of spectators, and a sea of flashing lights. At the center of it all was Brady, just a season after stepping up as the Patriots' starting quarterback.

The New England Patriots were facing off against the St. Louis Rams, the "Greatest Show on Turf," in Super Bowl XXXVI. The Rams were the favorites, with their explosive offense and seasoned players. Against them stood the Patriots, led by the young and relatively untested Brady. Yet, in Brady's mind, there was no room for doubt.

The weight of expectation, the noise of the crowd, the knowledge that millions were watching. Yet, amidst the chaos, Brady found serenity. "In those moments, you need to find your inner calm," he would later recount. "You need to drown out the noise and focus on what's important: the game."

As the final quarter was about to end, the scores were tied at 17-17. The Patriots had the ball with just 1:21 left on the clock. It was here that Brady showcased his mettle. With a calmness that seemed surprising for someone his age, he led his team down the field. His precision, focus, and determination were laser-sharp. Every throw, every decision, a testament to his mental toughness.

The Patriots edged closer to field goal range, and as the clock ticked down, Brady completed a crucial 23-yard pass. Now in range, they called upon their kicker, Adam Vinatieri, to attempt the 48-yard field goal.

The collective breath held by fans all over the world. Vinatieri stepped up, swung his leg, and the ball sailed through the uprights. The Patriots had done it! They had won their first Super Bowl, and Brady, the 24-year-old, the 199th draft pick, was named Super Bowl MVP.

On February 3, 2002, a young Brady led the Patriots to a victory over the Rams in Super Bowl XXXVI, securing the title of MVP. That win was just the start of his decorated career. He went on to lead the Patriots to victory again in Super Bowl XXXVIII against the Carolina Panthers, earning his second MVP award. A year later, Brady achieved a third victory in Super Bowl XXXIX, against the Philadelphia Eagles, marking his third Super Bowl ring in four years and earning another MVP title. These years were a testament to Brady's determination, hard work, and passion, establishing him as one of the greatest quarterbacks in NFL history.

In 2006, at the height of his career, Brady met Gisele Bündchen, the Brazilian supermodel who would become his wife and greatest cheerleader. Introduced by a mutual friend, they hit it off instantly and were married in 2009. Gisele not only supported Brady in his career but also introduced him to a lifestyle focusing on nutrition, mental wellness, and physical fitness, which greatly influenced his performance and longevity in football. For Brady, Gisele was more than a partner; she helped him grow and become a better version of himself.

In early 2009, our hero found himself confronted by his first major adversity on the field in the form of a season-ending knee injury. Imagine the crushing disappointment, the fears, the uncertainty - all crashing down in that single moment. Yet, in true Brady fashion, he refused to be defeated.

Upon his return to the field on September 7, 2009, he dazzled fans and critics alike, earning the title of AFC Offensive Player of the Week. This triumphant return was a testament to Brady's mental fortitude and his determination to overcome adversity.

In 2010, Brady was named the NFL's Comeback Player of the Year, a testament to his successful recovery from his knee injury. He threw for 4,398 passing yards and 28 touchdowns in his first season back, demonstrating that he was still at the top of his game.

However, Brady's trials were far from over. In 2015, the football world was rocked by the Deflategate scandal. Accused of manipulating game balls during a playoff game, Brady was handed a four-game suspension by the NFL. Despite appeals, the decision was upheld. Brady, a man known for his fierce competitiveness and commitment to fair play, found himself at the center of a controversy.

Brady returned to the field on October 9, 2016, following his suspension. Performing remarkably well, he led the Patriots to a resounding 33-13 win over Cleveland. The stats of the game spoke for themselves: 28 for 40 for 406 yards and three touchdowns.

The Super Bowl LI in 2017, the New England Patriots, trailing by a whopping 25 points against the Atlanta Falcons. The mood among Patriots fans was somber, the atmosphere heavy with impending defeat. But there was one man who didn't share this sense of dread - one man who still believed in victory, despite the seemingly impossible odds. His name? Tom Brady.

"The only thing you can do is play one play at a time," Brady once said. "You can't worry about the next play or the next quarter. You just focus on what you can control." And that's exactly what he did on that fateful day.

With relentless focus and determination, Brady orchestrated one of the most memorable comebacks in Super Bowl history. Down 28-3 in the third quarter, Brady brought the Patriots back from the brink. Pass by pass, touchdown by touchdown, he chipped away at the Falcons' lead. He guided the team, injecting a new sense of hope with each play.

In the final quarter, with mere minutes left on the clock, Brady threw a perfect pass to wide receiver Julian Edelman for the game-tying touchdown, forcing the game into overtime - a first in Super Bowl history. Then, in overtime, Brady drove the team 75 yards down the field to score the winning touchdown, securing a 34-28 victory for the Patriots. The impossible had been achieved.

The lessons of this iconic 28-3 comeback continue to inspire players and fans alike - reminding us all to never give up, no matter how grim the circumstances may seem.

In 2020, Brady, after 20 years with the Patriots, joined the Tampa Bay Buccaneers. This risky decision surprised many but showcased his desire for new challenges. In 2021, at 43, he won his seventh Super Bowl with the Buccaneers, a victory that solidified his legacy and defied age norms. Despite being viewed as underdogs in the final against Kansas City Chiefs, Brady led the Buccaneers to a resounding 31-9 victory, making him the oldest quarterback to win a Super Bowl.

This triumph reaffirmed his commitment to embracing new challenges and demonstrated the power of determination and self-belief in achieving greatness, regardless of age.

Let us end Brady's journey with some intriguing stories from his life.

As a young boy, Brady's first job was delivering newspapers in his hometown, San Mateo, an early testament to his diligence and sense of responsibility. Notably, he was also an accomplished baseball player, drafted by the Montreal Expos, showcasing his athletic versatility.

Throughout his career, Brady held onto his original shoulder pads from his debut at Michigan in 1995, indicative of his sentimental and superstitious side. His innovative training regimen, favoring resistance bands over traditional weights, exemplifies his willingness to break from convention.

Off the field, Brady's playful nature, often engaging in locker room pranks, highlighted the importance he placed on camaraderie and team spirit.

On February 1, 2023, at the age of 45, Brady announced his retirement from football, marking the end of a significant era in the sport. His legacy extends beyond statistics and records, epitomizing dedication, perseverance, and the relentless pursuit of excellence. His journey, from a paperboy to a legendary NFL quarterback, continues to inspire future generations. As he once said, "Football is a sport, but it's also a way of life," - a statement that perfectly encapsulates his enduring legacy.

MUHAMMAD ALI "THE GREATEST"

As the sun dipped low in the horizon, a frail yet determined man practiced his punch one last time. It was Muhammad Ali, known as the 'Louisville Lip' for his quick wit and sharp tongue. Even though Parkinson's disease had stolen his nimbleness and rapid-fire speech, the fire in his eyes was unquenched.

His wife, Lonnie, looked at him, her eyes shining. "Are you sure about this, Ali?" she asked, worried. "Lonnie, this is my last fight, and I need to do it," Ali said, his voice much softer than the loud one that used to fill boxing rings all over. Even though his body shook, his fist was strong. "I'm still the greatest!" He said with a brave smile, repeating what he always believed.

His last time in the public was at the start of the 1996 Olympic Games. He would hold the torch and, in his own words, "Show the world that I'm still fighting." This moment showed his strong spirit and his life lesson: "Don't count the days, make the days count."

When people around the world saw him light the Olympic torch, they saw a fighter who was still winning, in his own way. His famous saying - "Float like a butterfly, sting like a bee" - reminded people that even when life is tough, being strong and brave can help you win.

On a cold morning of January 17, 1942, in Louisville, Kentucky, a boy was born to Cassius Clay Sr. and Odessa O'Grady Clay. They named him Cassius Marcellus Clay Jr., a name that would become legendary in boxing.

The Clays weren't rich. Cassius Sr., a sign painter, had a hard time providing for his family. Despite this, their home was always full of life. Young Cassius grew up with his brother, Rudy, in a neighborhood filled with laughter and music.

Cassius was a lively boy with a contagious laugh and lots of charm. As a child, he saw a boxing match on TV and was fascinated. He began to pretend-box, showing early signs of his future passion.

Their home, though poor, was full of love and joy. His parents taught him about hard work, resilience, and kindness. These values would later shape Cassius's future.

His parents' wisdom, "Cassius, it's not the size of the man, but the size of his heart that matters," and "Son, it's not about how hard you can hit. It's about how hard you can get hit and keep moving forward," guided Cassius on his journey to becoming Muhammad Ali.

On an ordinary day in 1954, an event happened that was anything but ordinary.

It was a day that would set in motion the journey of a young boy from Louisville into the most prestigious records of boxing history. It all started with a stolen bicycle.

12-year-old Cassius loved his red-and-white Schwinn bicycle. He considered it his prized possession, a symbol of freedom and adventure. He would pedal through the streets of his neighborhood, his laughter trailing behind him like a joyful song. But one afternoon, Cassius returned from a local bazaar to find his beloved bicycle missing.

Cassius was heartbroken, his young heart throbbing with a sense of injustice. Frustration clouded his eyes as he stomped around, trying to locate his stolen treasure. A sympathetic passerby noticed his distress and directed him to a nearby police station where Officer Joe Martin, who also happened to run a local boxing gym, was on duty.

Martin recalled the moment when young Cassius burst into the station, tears welling up in his eyes, fists clenched, declaring, "I'm gonna whup whoever stole my bike!" The policeman, seeing an opportunity, simply responded, "Well, you better learn how to fight before you start challenging people."

Cassius looked up at Martin, a spark in his eyes. The next day, Cassius showed up at Martin's gym, ready to channel his anger and disappointment into something constructive. Martin saw a fire in Cassius that day, an inner spark that would later ignite into a boxing legend.

Even as an adult, Muhammad Ali would recall this incident, humor dancing in his eyes as he'd say, "Whoever stole that bike, I'm thankful to them. They didn't realize they were stealing me a future!" It was this unexpected twist of fate, spun from a stolen bicycle, that propelled Cassius into the world of boxing, forever changing his life's trajectory.

The local boxing gym was a new place for young Cassius Clay. It was full of the smells of leather gloves, sweat, and the sound of punches hitting bags. Here, Cassius felt alive and full of energy. At the center of it all was Joe Martin, the police officer who guided him towards boxing.

Martin was a tough coach who spotted Cassius's talent and potential. He took Cassius and trained him, turning his natural ability into disciplined skills.

Martin wasn't just a boxing coach to Cassius but also a mentor. He taught him that boxing wasn't just about physical strength, but also about mental strength and the ability to keep going even when things get hard.

Cassius would go to the gym every day after school. He learned to punch and move around the boxing ring, and Martin taught him to work hard, be disciplined, and never give up.

One day, Cassius asked Martin why boxing was so hard. Martin replied, "Because, Cassius, being a champion isn't easy. You've got to fight for it."

Years later, Muhammad Ali would remember his early days with Martin, saying, "Martin made me run extra miles when I wanted to quit, he made me spar when I was tired. He made me a fighter. He made me Muhammad Ali."

Under Joe Martin, young Cassius quickly became a good boxer. He trained hard, learned about boxing, and dreamt of winning. With time, Cassius changed from a boy into a strong young fighter. Martin thought Cassius was ready for his first amateur fight, which started his boxing career.

His first fight was in 1954, just after he turned twelve. A small crowd came to watch the young boxers. Cassius got into the ring, his heart beating fast. Martin told him, "Remember, Cassius, in the ring, it's not just about fighting, it's about dancing."

Cassius moved in the ring with grace and speed. His punches were precise and skilled. That night, Cassius won his first match, fueling his desire to reach the top of boxing.

Cassius kept winning in the amateur boxing world and quickly rose up the ranks. His unique style and precise punches earned him respect. His big moment was when he won the Golden Gloves Tournament for novices in 1956 in the light heavyweight division. This was the world's first look at the future "The Greatest."

Ali often remembered his early boxing years, saying, "I was dancing and dodging, weaving and jabbing. I was a kid, but I was on fire. I knew then, I was born to box."

In 1960, a young Cassius Clay joined the US Olympic boxing team after several big wins. He was going to Rome, Italy, for the 1960 Summer Olympics. Cassius was both excited and nervous. As he got on the plane to Rome, he held a small American flag, feeling proud and hopeful.

He often remembered this moment, saying, "I was a boy from Kentucky, going to fight for my country. I wasn't just fighting for myself anymore, but for every American."

In Rome, Cassius faced tough competitors. But he didn't back down. His determination grew even stronger. Cassius fought with skill and agility, outperforming his competitors.

He made it to the final match against Zbigniew Pietrzykowski from Poland. After a tough fight, Cassius won and earned the gold medal in the light heavyweight boxing division. He felt pride and joy standing on the podium with a gold medal around his neck. This moment marked a big change in his life.

Years later, Ali would say, "Standing on that podium, I felt like a king. I was no longer just Cassius Clay, I was Ali, the Olympic Champion."

After winning an Olympic gold medal, Cassius came back home and decided to become a professional boxer. A group of businessmen from Louisville sponsored him and he began training with a new coach, Angelo Dundee.

Ali once said about this time, "I had to be faster, stronger, and smarter. Dundee pushed me harder than ever, but I was ready. I wanted to be the greatest."

Under Dundee's strict guidance, Clay became an even better boxer. He learned new strategies and how to use his words as well as his fists. He was quick and precise, ready to compete professionally.

On October 29, 1960, Clay had his first professional boxing match against Tunney Hunsaker. Clay won easily, showing off his speed and agility. This victory made him popular with fans. He was not just a boxer, he was also a showman, often entertaining people with his clever words before a match.

Later as Ali, he would look back on these days proudly, saying, "I floated like a butterfly, and stung like a bee. Nobody could lay a glove on me."

February 25, 1964, would forever be marked as a red-letter day in boxing history. The location was Miami Beach, Florida, and the event was a clash of titans. Cassius Clay, now a rising star in the professional boxing world, was about to face the reigning heavyweight champion, Sonny Liston, in a fight that was poised to shake the boxing world to its core.

Liston, with his imposing physique and powerful punches, was considered invincible. But Clay was unfazed. "I'm young; I'm handsome; I'm fast. I can't possibly be beat," he declared, full of his usual bravado.

The pre-fight press conference was a spectacle, with Clay shouting predictions and rhymes, creating chaos. He used the phrase, "Float like a butterfly, sting like a bee," unsettling his opponent, Liston, with his theatrics.

In the fight, Clay's speed and agility were too much for Liston, who missed punch after punch. After six rounds, Liston, exhausted and injured, forfeited the match.

Clay's victory over Liston made him the world heavyweight champion at 22. Celebrating in the ring, he shouted, "I shocked the world! I am the greatest!" This was not just a boxing match, but a testament to Clay's determination and self-belief.

Days after defeating Liston, Cassius Clay revealed his conversion to Islam, adopting the name Muhammad Ali.

"I believe in Islam. I believe in Allah and peace... I'm not Christian anymore," he declared.

This was more than a name change; it was a declaration of faith and identity, sparking controversy. Predominantly Christian America struggled to accept a Muslim Heavyweight Champion. Despite this, the media often used his birth name, which Ali refuted, insisting on being called Muhammad Ali.

Despite the backlash, Ali stood firm, challenging societal norms. When asked about his decision, he confidently said, "I know where I'm going, and I know the truth. I don't have to be what you want me to be. I'm free to be what I want.

It was 1967, and the Vietnam War was raging. When called upon to serve his country, Muhammad Ali did the unthinkable - he refused. His reason was clear, "My conscience won't let me go shoot my brother, or some darker people, or some poor, hungry people in the mud for big, powerful America." This defiance resulted in his arrest and the subsequent stripping of his heavyweight boxing titles.

Ali's refusal was grounded in his religious beliefs and his unwavering commitment to the principles of justice and equality. He was viewed by some as unpatriotic, yet by others, he was hailed as a beacon of courage and conviction.

His refusal to be drafted into the army triggered a series of legal battles. Ali was determined to clear his name and return to the ring, and he fought for his cause in court with the same zeal he displayed in the boxing ring.

"I ain't draft dodging. I ain't burning no flag, and I ain't running to Canada. I'm staying right here," Ali proclaimed, "You want to send me to jail? Fine, you go right ahead. I've been in jail for 400 years. I could be there for 4 or 5 more, but I ain't going no 10,000 miles to help murder and kill other poor people. If I want to die, I'll die right here, right now, fighting you."

In 1971, after years of legal wrangling, the Supreme Court overturned his conviction, marking a victory for Ali. His steadfastness in standing up for his beliefs and rights had paid off.

The legal battles were behind him, and Muhammad Ali was on a mission to reclaim what was rightfully his - the World Heavyweight Championship. His comeback fight against Jerry Quarry in 1970 was a demonstration of Ali's undiminished prowess. However, the match that was on everyone's lips was Ali versus Joe Frazier, the reigning champion who had taken the throne during Ali's absence.

The much-anticipated "Fight of the Century" took place on March 8, 1971, at Madison Square Garden. The world watched as the deposed king, Ali, sought to reclaim his crown from the current champion, Frazier.

In the lead-up to the fight, Ali's charisma was in full display. His psychological warfare, a mix of humorous taunts and pointed jibes, was aimed at unsettling Frazier. "Frazier is too ugly to be champ. The world champ should be pretty like me!" Ali quipped, revealing his humorous side even amidst the heated rivalry.

The match itself was nothing short of spectacular. Both fighters left nothing in the tank, battling it out over fifteen grueling rounds. Ali danced around the ring, landing precise and powerful punches, while Frazier relentlessly pursued Ali, his devastating left hook a constant menace. In the end, Frazier retained the title, and Ali tasted professional defeat for the first time.

Yet, defeat did not tarnish Ali's spirit. He graciously accepted the loss, saying, "We both fought a good fight. Joe's a tough man, and I miscalculated him. I'll be back." True to his word, Ali did come back, setting up a series of iconic rematches with Frazier and proving that he was a champion, regardless of the outcome.

Muhammad Ali faced formidable opponent George Foreman in 1974 in a boxing match known as the "Rumble in the Jungle." Despite Foreman's youth and strength, Ali utilized a strategy called "rope-a-dope," where he allowed Foreman to throw punches while Ali leaned against the ropes to absorb the blows and tire Foreman out. In the eighth round, Ali seized the opportunity to attack an exhausted Foreman, resulting in Foreman falling and Ali reclaiming his World Heavyweight Champion title.

A year later, on October 1, 1975, Ali faced Joe Frazier in their third and final face-off, known as the "Thrilla in Manila." The brutal fight was a test of endurance, with both boxers giving and receiving severe punishment.

After 14 intense rounds, Ali launched a powerful attack on Frazier that caused Frazier's eyes to swell and limit his vision.

Frazier's corner decided to end the fight before the 15th round, resulting in Ali winning by a technical knockout. Despite the fierce competition, Ali showed immense respect for Frazier, acknowledging that Frazier brought out the best in him.

Muhammad Ali, after his victory in the "Thrilla in Manila" over Joe Frazier, became a global sensation as a boxing legend and an influential figure beyond the sport. Known for his charisma, defiant spirit, and advocacy for social justice, Ali's impact grew even after his boxing career wound down.

Despite facing adversities such as Parkinson's disease, he remained committed to various causes and continued to inspire millions. His legacy is remembered not only for his athletic prowess as a three-time heavyweight champion but also for his immense courage, compassion, and conviction in uniting people through faith and love.

Ali's life story serves as a powerful reminder that true greatness extends beyond winning titles—it's about making a difference in the world.

RONDA ROUSEY "ROWDY"

In the glimmering arena, brimming with fans from all corners of the globe, Ronda Rousey stood face to face with her opponent, Liz Carmouche. Liz was a fearsome competitor, widely respected for her powerful strikes and formidable toughness. But the night of February 23, 2013, was no ordinary night. It was UFC 157, a historic event that marked the first-ever women's fight in the Ultimate Fighting Championship's history.

The electric energy of the spectators filled the arena, their anxious eyes watching the two warriors in the octagon. Ronda and Liz. The anticipation was palpable. After years of sweat, determination, and unyielding grit, Ronda was here, under the spotlight, ready to carve her name into the history of the UFC.

The referee's whistle echoed, signaling the start of the monumental fight. Ronda's heart pounded like a drum as she squared off against Liz. The first few minutes were a whirlwind of strikes and kicks, each fighter looking for an opening. Liz, strong and unyielding, was proving to be a tough opponent. But Ronda, with her unwavering focus and indomitable spirit, held her ground.

The fight escalated quickly. Liz tried to surprise Ronda with a rear-naked choke, but Ronda, as if carrying the essence of her mantra, remained unyielding. She fought back, eventually escaping the choke and flipping the game on Liz.

Then, with a swift and practiced move, Ronda seized her chance. She caught Liz in her infamous armbar, a move she had perfected over the years. Liz struggled, but the grip was unbreakable. With no other option, Liz tapped out. And just like that, after four intense minutes and 49 seconds, Ronda was declared the victor.

Ronda stood up, her breaths heavy but her spirit soaring. The crowd went wild, their cheers echoing around the arena. As the shining championship belt was wrapped around her waist, Ronda smiled, her triumph clear in her shining eyes. She had done it. She had made history. She looked at the crowd, her gaze sweeping over the sea of cheering fans, and repeated the mantra that had carried her this far: "No one has the right to beat you." And in that moment, she was not only a champion but a symbol of perseverance and strength.

On February 1, 1987, in the quiet town of Riverside, California, a future champion was born. Ronda Jean Rousey entered the world not with a whimper but a roar, her life's journey marked by challenges right from the start. Born with her umbilical cord wrapped around her neck, Ronda developed apraxia, a language disorder that made it difficult for her to speak.

Ronda's early years were spent in a silent world. While other kids her age were learning to voice their thoughts, Ronda was struggling to form words. It was a challenge, yes, but one that she tackled head-on. It was in these early years that Ronda developed her fighting spirit, her refusal to be kept down.

It wasn't easy. There were times when frustration crept in, when her inability to speak felt like a mountain she couldn't climb. But Ronda, even as a child, was a fighter. She refused to let her condition define her or limit her potential. In her own words, she would later say, "I am not a do-nothing girl."

Even as a young girl, Ronda Rousey was no stranger to the world of martial arts. Her mother, AnnMaria De Mars, was a judo champion in her own right—the first American to win a World Judo Championship. It was under her mother's watchful eye and tutelage that Ronda was introduced to judo. But it wasn't just any form of training, it was therapy—a way for Ronda to build confidence, to find her voice in the throws and grapples of judo.

The training was as unconventional as it was intense. Imagine being woken up from a deep slumber, not by an alarm clock or the morning sunlight peeking through your window, but by your mother initiating a surprise armbar attack. That was Ronda's reality. Her mornings were not filled with yawns and stretch, but armbars and takedowns. But rather than deterring her, these surprise morning attacks instilled in Ronda a fighting spirit. They taught her to be ready, to be alert—lessons that would later become invaluable in her career.

The training wasn't easy, nor was it always fun. The early morning wake-up attacks, the endless hours spent perfecting techniques—it was grueling. But Ronda was relentless. She was not training just to fight; she was training to become a champion, a fighter in every sense of the word.

Her mother's training was tough, but it was also empowering. It was in the judo hall that Ronda discovered her love for martial arts, her passion for competition. She learned not just to fight, but to fight with a purpose, with a drive. Judo became a lifeline, a tool to overcome her struggles. It gave her a sense of control, a way to communicate when words failed her.

A judoka is a person who practices judo, a modern martial art and combat sport that originated in Japan. Judo translates to "the gentle way," which reflects its philosophy of using an opponent's strength against them. The goal in judo is to either throw or take down an adversary to the ground, immobilize them with a pin, or force them to submit with a joint lock or a choke.

Her transition from a quiet girl to a judoka was symbolic of her growth, both physically and mentally, shaping her into a strong, confident individual who would later create history in the world of combat sports.

Ronda's journey from the judo mats in her mother's training hall to the bright lights of the UFC octagon wasn't a solitary one. Along the way, she was guided by a series of influential coaches who helped mold her into the world-class fighter she became.

After her mother, Ronda's journey led her to the Hayastan MMA Academy, where she trained under the watchful eyes of Gokor Chivichyan and Gene LeBell. Gokor, an accomplished judoka, and Gene, a legend in the world of judo and professional wrestling, were instrumental in shaping Ronda's fighting style.

Ronda's training regime under Gokor and Gene was grueling and intense. The duo didn't just focus on her physical strength and technical skills; they also honed her mental agility and strategic thinking. Ronda trained tirelessly, learning and mastering a range of techniques, from armbars and chokes to punches, kicks and takedowns. Her coaches pushed her to her limits, but Ronda was no stranger to hard work. She thrived under the pressure, the exhaustion fueling her determination to succeed.

Training under Gokor and Gene, Ronda began to develop her unique fighting style, a blend of power, speed, and technique that would later become her trademark. She adopted Gene's catchphrase, "The only way to the top is by persistent, intelligent, hard work," and lived by it, pushing herself to achieve more, to become better.

In addition to the intensive training, Ronda also competed in numerous judo tournaments, earning a reputation as a formidable opponent. Her victories in these competitions were a testament to her talent, her coaches' teachings, and her relentless pursuit of excellence.

Ronda's training wasn't just about physical prowess; it was about developing a winning mentality. Her coaches taught her to be fearless, to face her opponents with confidence and determination. They instilled in her a warrior's spirit, a burning desire to win.

Her journey in judo was marked by several remarkable milestones, each one a testament to her talent, her determination, and her relentless spirit. After years of rigorous training, countless competitions, and an unyielding dedication, Ronda's hard work paid off in a big way when she qualified for the 2004 Olympic Games in Athens at the tender age of 17.

This achievement made her the youngest judoka to participate in the Olympics, a significant feat that echoed her prowess in the sport.

However, her journey didn't stop there. Following Athens, Ronda continued to train and compete fiercely, her eyes set on a bigger goal—the 2008 Olympic Games in Beijing. As the world watched, Ronda once again stepped onto the global stage, competing against the best judokas from across the globe.

The competition was intense, but Ronda was undeterred. She faced each opponent with the same focus and determination that had carried her through her training and past tournaments. One by one, she bested her opponents, advancing through the ranks. The culmination of her journey came when Ronda clinched the bronze medal in judo, making her the first American woman to win an Olympic medal in the sport.

Her victory in Beijing was more than just a personal achievement. It was a historic moment that redefined the narrative for women in judo, particularly American women. Ronda had not just won a medal; she had broken barriers and shattered ceilings. She had made history.

Reflecting on her historic win, Ronda later said, "Every single second of hard work was worth it. I'm happy I did things the hard way, and I'm proud to be the kind of person who has the courage to not take the easy road."

Following her success in judo, Ronda Rousey set her sights on a new arena - Mixed Martial Arts (MMA). Her transition into MMA wasn't just a career shift; it was a move that would redefine women's participation in the sport.

After a brief stint in amateur MMA, where she had a flawless 3-0 record, Ronda turned professional, fighting in the Strikeforce. Her dominance was immediate and undeniable. Within a year, Ronda captured the Strikeforce Women's Bantamweight Championship with her signature armbar submission, displaying a level of technique and agility that left fans and critics in awe.

But Ronda wasn't satisfied with just being a champion in Strikeforce. She had her eyes set on the Ultimate Fighting Championship (UFC), the biggest stage in MMA. However, there was one problem - the UFC didn't have women's divisions.

In a conversation with Dana White, the president of the UFC, Ronda made a case for women fighters. She passionately argued for their inclusion, stating that women were just as capable and deserving as men in the octagon.

Her relentless advocacy paid off when Dana White finally announced the establishment of the Women's Bantamweight Division, with Ronda as its first champion.

Ronda's first UFC fight was a landmark moment, not just for her, but for women in MMA. She faced Liz Carmouche in an intense, adrenaline-pumping match. Displaying her now-famous armbar submission, Ronda emerged victorious, defending her Bantamweight Championship title.

Her reign in the UFC was nothing short of spectacular. Ronda defended her title six times, a reign that lasted 1,074 days. Her fights were marked by rapid-fire victories, often won in the first round itself.

This era of dominance not only solidified her status as a world-class fighter but also brought unprecedented attention to women's divisions in the UFC.

Reflecting on her journey, Ronda once said, "People say to me all the time, 'You have no fear.' I tell them, 'No, that's not true. I'm scared all the time. You have to have fear in order to have courage. I'm a courageous person because I'm a scared person.'"

From being a trailblazer in judo to creating waves in MMA and UFC, Ronda Rousey's journey has been a powerful narrative of courage, determination, and resilience. She didn't just win fights; she fought for change, paving the way for future generations of women fighters.

Ronda Rousey's illustrious career is studded with numerous accolades, achievements, and career-defining moments. One of her standout fights where without a doubt UFC 184.

The match was against Cat Zingano on February 28, 2015, at the Staples Center in Los Angeles, California, and was a battle of giants. The anticipation was electric, and the atmosphere in the arena was thick with excitement. Fans packed the venue, sporting Rousey's merchandise, waving banners, and eagerly discussing the impending showdown between two of the sport's most formidable competitors.

As the lights dimmed, and Rousey made her way to the cage, a roar erupted from the crowd. Her laser-focused expression told a story of determination and readiness, while her confident stride seemed to embody her reign as the UFC Women's Bantamweight Champion.

Once inside the cage, the referee's whistle signalled the start, and the fighters engaged. Zingano charged in immediately with an aggressive flying knee attempt, looking to catch Rousey off guard. But Rousey, known for her judo expertise, instinctively caught her opponent and seamlessly transitioned into her signature armbar submission hold.

Ronda's achievements weren't limited to the UFC octagon. In recognition of her outstanding contributions to the sport, Ronda was inducted into the UFC Hall of Fame in 2018, making her the first woman to receive this honor. This induction wasn't just a personal victory for Ronda; it was a triumph for all women in the sport, a testament to her trailblazing influence on women's MMA.

Ronda's influence extended beyond the confines of the MMA world. In 2015, Sports Illustrated named her the World's Most Dominant Athlete, acknowledging her dominance and influence across all sports, not just MMA. The following year, she appeared on the cover of the magazine's Swimsuit Issue, a testament to her increasing popularity and cultural influence.

In addition to these accolades, Ronda was also named the Female Fighter of the Year in 2012, 2013, and 2014 by the World MMA Awards. Furthermore, she bagged the ESPY Award for Best Fighter, outshining male counterparts, in 2015.

Never one to rest on her laurels, Ronda's adventurous spirit took her beyond the world of MMA and UFC to new arenas – professional wrestling and acting.

In 2018, Ronda made her official WWE debut at the Royal Rumble. The former judoka and MMA fighter was now a professional wrestler, bringing the same passion and intensity to the ring as she did to the octagon. Her impressive performance led to a meteoric rise in WWE, culminating in her winning the Raw Women's Championship, further establishing her dominance in yet another combat sport.

Parallel to her wrestling career, Ronda also ventured into acting. She appeared in several films and television shows, including "The Expendables 3", "Furious 7", and "Blindspot", showcasing her versatility as an entertainer. Her roles often mirrored her real-life persona – tough, fearless, and tenacious, winning over audiences with her raw energy and charismatic performances.

Ronda's successful transition into WWE and acting underscored her multifaceted talent and adaptability. As she put it, "Change is not always a bad thing. It can be beautiful and exciting." These new ventures were proof of Ronda's ability to embrace change and excel in whatever path she chose, highlighting her unyielding spirit and persistent pursuit of new challenges.

Ronda faced many challenges in her life. She had to deal with the tragic suicide of her father. In 1995, he broke his back while sledding with his daughters.

The injury caused him to become a paraplegic, and he was given a prognosis of only a few years to live.

Struggling with the pain and the realization of his deteriorating health, Ronald Rousey took his own life later that year. His death had a profound impact on Ronda and her family.

She also admits to struggling with depression after losing to Holly Holm at UFC 193 for the first time in her life while disappearing from public view. But she overcame these challenges and used them to fuel her determination throughout her life.

Ronda is also known for her love of animals. She has a ranch filled with various farm animals from cows, to goats and dogs. She even worked at an animal rehabilitation center during one of her training sessions.

She has worked as a bartender, waitress, and canine physical therapy assistant. She even dropped out of high school to focus on her training, although she later earned her General Education Diploma (GED).

As well as appearing in films and TV shows, she was the first female athlete to guest host ESPN's Sports Center. She was even featured on the cover of Australia's Men's Fitness Magazine, becoming the first woman to do so.

Ronda was given the nickname "Rowdy" by her friends, a name originally associated with the professional wrestler and Hall of Famer, Roddy Piper. At first, Ronda was hesitant to use the nickname "Rowdy" because she felt it might be disrespectful to the legendary Canadian wrestler. However, after meeting Piper in person, he gave his approval for her to use the name. This nickname is a testament to Ronda's fighting spirit and her success in the wrestling industry, mirroring the reputation of the great Roddy Piper. So, Ronda "Rowdy" Rousey continues to inspire many with her strength, determination, and respect for the history of her sport. Despite her success, Ronda has remained humble.

Let's end the story with a final quote from Ronda herself that encapsulates her spirit, "You have to fight because you can't count on anyone else fighting for you."

SHAUN WHITE "THE FLYING TOMATO"

It was 2018 Winter Olympics in Pyeongchang, South Korea. The biting cold of winter hung in the air, and a sense of electric anticipation rippled through the crowd. The Halfpipe Snowboarding event was on, and all eyes are on one man – Shaun White.

He stands poised at the starting point, snowboard under his feet, the icy slope of the halfpipe stretching out before him. His red hair, peeking out from under his helmet, has earned him the nickname "The Flying Tomato," but today, he looks more like a lion ready to pounce.

With a deep breath, Shaun launches into his final run. The crowd goes silent as he rockets down the halfpipe, then shoots up the other side. He twists in the air, executing complex flips and turns with remarkable ease. He lands perfectly and repeats the sequence, one airborne maneuver after the next, soaring even higher. The crowd roars in disbelief and admiration.

His performance is flawless, each trick executed with incredible precision and style. As he makes his final landing, the crowd erupts into cheers. Shaun White has done it again - he has won his third Olympic gold medal in the Halfpipe event, scoring a perfect 100!

Clutching his snowboard, Shaun looks at the cheering crowd, a broad smile spreading across his face. He pumps his fist into the air, exhilaration and victory reflecting in his eyes. In that moment, he is not just Shaun White, the snowboarder. He became a symbol of perseverance, determination, and the realization of a dream that seemed almost unattainable. In his own words, he would later describe the feeling saying, "I've never been more focused and driven." Little did everyone know, this moment of triumph was the culmination of a journey that had started many years ago, in a little town in San Diego, California.

On September 3, 1986, a baby boy named Shaun Roger White was born to Cathy and Roger White in San Diego, California. He was the youngest of four kids, and even from a birth, Shaun experienced challenges. He was born with a heart that was a little different than most others. He had a condition called Tetralogy of Fallot, a congenital heart defect that made his little heart work much harder than it should have.

Before he could even walk, Shaun had to face something scarier than any halfpipe or steep slope. He underwent not one, but two open-heart surgeries all before his first birthday. But, if you think this made him weak or scared, you would be wrong. Shaun, even as a baby, was a fighter. He took each day as it came, and with the love and support of his family, he powered through.

His parents often said that Shaun's early challenges made him stronger. His fighting spirit shone through, helping him to tackle any hurdle that life threw at him.

As Shaun grew older, he discovered two sports that would change his life forever: skateboarding and snowboarding. Even as a tiny kid, Shaun had a natural flair for balance and speed. His first love was skateboarding. He would spend hours at the local skate park, practicing tricks and flips, his small size belying his tremendous talent.

One day, while Shaun was mastering his kickflips, a famous skateboarder named Tony Hawk spotted him. Hawk, impressed by Shaun's skills and determination, took the young boy under his wing. Under Hawk's mentorship, Shaun's skateboarding abilities rapidly improved, his natural talent complemented by Hawk's expertise.

Shaun's journey took an interesting turn when he was introduced to snowboarding. At the tender age of six, Shaun strapped on a snowboard for the first time, replacing his wheels for snow. Trading the skateboard parks of San Diego for the snowy slopes of Big Bear, Shaun found a new love in snowboarding. He quickly transitioned from the board to the slopes, taking to the snow like a fish to water. His remarkable skill at such a young age did not go unnoticed, and he received his first sponsorship when he was just seven years old.

Shaun's parents often drove him for hours to the ski resorts, watching from the bottom as their little boy weaved magic on the snow. Despite the long hours and cold weather, Shaun always had a smile on his face. He loved the feeling of speed and the thrill of performing high flying tricks on his snowboard. It was during these early years that Shaun discovered his passion for snowboarding, a passion that would eventually lead him to unimaginable heights.

In an interview, Shaun once recalled these early years and said, "I fell in love with the freedom of snowboarding, the freedom to create your path down the mountain, your own tricks and maneuvers. It was about breaking boundaries, pushing limits, and it was about fun." Little did the young Shaun know, he was setting himself on a path that would take him from the skate parks of San Diego to the snowy peaks of the Winter Olympics.

While Shaun's heart belonged to the snow-capped peaks, he never lost his passion for skateboarding. In fact, he would become as iconic on the board as he was on the slopes. Under Tony Hawk's guidance, Shaun honed his skateboarding skills, swiftly making a name for himself in the skateboarding circuit too.

Shaun's fearless approach and incredible talent made him a force to be reckoned with on the ramps. He performed tricks and flips that left spectators and competitors astounded. His feats were not just about winning; they were about redefining the limits of what was possible on a skateboard.

At just 16 years old, Shaun turned professional. He was no longer the small boy practicing kickflips in the skate park; he was now the professional skateboarder. His reputation grew with each competition, and before long, he was not just competing in tournaments, but also winning them. His high-flying tricks and fearless approach earned him various titles in skateboarding competitions, making him one of the youngest champions in the sport.

Shaun's success in skateboarding was about more than just talent; it was his dedication and love for the sport. Despite the pressures of competing at a professional level, Shaun always maintained a positive attitude.

As impressive as Shaun's skateboarding achievements were, it was on the snow-covered slopes where he truly made history. The snow was his canvas, and with his snowboard as his brush, Shaun was ready to paint a masterpiece.

Shaun's first major competition was the Winter X Games in 2003, held in Aspen, Colorado, a tournament that would become synonymous with his name in the years to come. Shaun, with his bright red hair flying behind him, sped down the slopes, his snowboard carving graceful arcs in the snow. His performances were nothing short of spectacular, earning him gold medals in both the superpipe and slopestyle events.

The X Games is an annual extreme sports event hosted, produced, and broadcast by ESPN. The competition, which started in 1995, features athletes from around the globe who compete in various extreme sports, including skateboarding, BMX, Moto X, and snowboarding, among others.

The X Games are split into two major events: the Summer X Games and the Winter X Games. The Summer X Games primarily focus on street sports like skateboarding and BMX, while the Winter X Games feature winter sports like snowboarding and skiing.

The competition is famous for its high-flying, daring stunts, and tricks performed by some of the world's best extreme athletes. The X Games have played a significant role in the growth and promotion of extreme sports, offering a platform for athletes to compete at a high level and gain international recognition.

Shaun, with his impressive performances in snowboarding and skateboarding, has been one of the standout athletes in the history of the X Games.

However, the stage where Shaun truly shined was the Winter Olympics in Torino, 2006. Despite being relatively new to the international scene, Shaun dazzled the world with his snowboarding prowess, winning gold in the halfpipe event. His signature moves, such as the Double McTwist 1260, left the spectators in awe.

But Shaun was far from done. Four years later, at the 2010 Vancouver Winter Olympics, he once again dominated the halfpipe event, winning his second consecutive gold medal. His performances were a blend of artistry and athleticism, a thrilling display of gravity-defying tricks and speed.

Yet, it was the 2018 Pyeongchang Winter Olympics that would etch Shaun's name into snowboarding's Hall of Fame. In the halfpipe event, Shaun faced tough competition from riders like Ayumu Hirano and Scotty James. But, as he had done time and again, Shaun rose to the challenge. His final run was a sight to behold, a perfect blend of precision, style, and daring. He executed back-to-back 1440-degree spins followed by a Sky Hook, a frontside double cork 1260, scoring an impressive 97.75. His triumphant win earned him his third Olympic gold medal in the halfpipe, a record-breaking achievement, and the 100th gold medal for the United States in Winter Games history. This performance further solidified his place as one of the greatest snowboarders of all time.

Shaun's achievements extend beyond the Olympics. He holds the record for the most X Games gold medals, and he is the first male athlete to win four consecutive gold medals in one discipline at the Winter X Games. He also won the prestigious Air & Style Contest in 2003 and 2004.

One of the most defining moments in Shaun White's career came in the winter of 2012 at the Winter X Games. On this day, Shaun didn't just win another medal or break another record. He did something no one had ever done before: he achieved a perfect score in the men's Snowboard Superpipe.

The stage was set. The crowd waited in anticipation as Shaun prepared for his final run. He had already secured the gold medal, but Shaun wasn't done. He had his sights set on a different kind of glory.

As Shaun dropped into the Superpipe, everyone held their breath. He launched himself into the air, twisting and flipping with a grace and fearlessness that had become his signature. One by one, he executed his tricks flawlessly, defying gravity with every move.

When Shaun finally touched down, the crowd erupted into applause. They knew they had just witnessed something special. But the biggest confirmation came when the judges revealed their scores: a perfect 100.

Shaun White had just made history.

The significance of this moment was not lost on Shaun. "This was a night I would remember forever," he said later. "Not just because of the perfect score, but because it showed me that even when you think you've reached the top, there's always another level to strive for."

Achieving a perfect score in the Snowboard Superpipe was more than just another accolade for Shaun White. It was a testament to his relentless pursuit of perfection, his unwavering commitment to pushing the boundaries of his sport, and his unquenchable thirst for greatness. Shaun White's perfect 100 is a symbol of his extraordinary career, a moment that encapsulates his ethos: to defy limits, break records, and to always, always strive for perfection.

Shaun's snowboarding career is filled with remarkable feats and record-breaking performances. His relentless drive and passion for the sport have made him one of the most decorated athletes in snowboarding history.

While Shaun White's snowboarding and skateboarding abilities are legendary, there are many facets to his personality and career.

When Shaun White isn't shredding snow on the slopes or grinding rails on his skateboard, he switches his board for a six-string – a guitar, to be exact. This snowboarding and skateboarding legend is also a passionate musician. His love for music is just as profound as his dedication to his athletic career.

Shaun was introduced to music at a young age, and it didn't take long for him to fall in love with it. Like his snowboarding, Shaun's approach to music is focused and committed. He spent countless hours strumming his guitar, slowly but surely honing his skills. He loves to share his passion for music, often seen jamming with friends and family.

But Shaun's musical journey didn't stop at casual jamming sessions. He took his passion to the next level when he became a part of a rock band called 'Bad Things.' Shaun and his bandmates, including childhood friends and experienced musicians, shared a common love for music and a vision for their band.

Despite his busy athletic schedule, Shaun devoted time to 'Bad Things.' The band composed and performed their songs, showcasing their talent at various events.

In 2013, they even had the honor of performing at Lollapalooza, a renowned music festival that features popular alternative rock, heavy metal, punk rock, hip hop, and electronic music bands and artists. Their performance was a hit, and Shaun's joy was visible as he strummed his guitar and swayed to the music.

Being part of 'Bad Things' provided Shaun with a creative outlet outside of sports. It allowed him to express himself in a different way and share a different side of his personality with his fans. When asked about his experience with 'Bad Things,' Shaun said, "Being in 'Bad Things' allows me to engage with my fans in a new way. I hope our music brings as much joy to people as snowboarding does to me."

So, while we know and love Shaun White for his breathtaking tricks on the snow and ramps, let's not forget the man behind the guitar, rocking to his own rhythm. His story reminds us that we can have more than one passion in life, and pursuing those passions is what makes life exciting and fulfilling. After all, as Shaun proves, who says a world-class athlete can't also be a rock star?

Sharing his passion for music, Shaun said, "Music, like snowboarding, is about expression and creativity. It's about sharing a part of yourself with the world."

Moreover, Shaun's influence extends to the world of video games. "Shaun White Snowboarding," a video game bearing his name and likeness, debuted in 2008. This game was not just another sports-themed offering. Shaun was deeply involved in its development, providing input and feedback to ensure the game captured the true essence of snowboarding. His goal was to create a game that felt as authentic as possible, one that mirrored the adrenaline, excitement, and creativity intrinsic to the sport.

When asked about the video game, Shaun said, "I wanted to create something that was true to snowboarding - the thrill, the creativity, the constant drive to challenge oneself. This game is not just about me, it's about the spirit of the sport."

"Shaun White Snowboarding" was a hit among fans and gamers, gaining positive reviews for its exciting gameplay and authentic representation of snowboarding. It served as another platform for Shaun to inspire young, aspiring snowboarders and instill in them the love for the sport.

But even beyond snowboarding, skateboarding, music, and video games, Shaun has also used his platform for good. He has been involved in various charitable activities, giving back to the community and using his fame to

114

make a difference. Shaun has partnered with St. Jude Children's Research Hospital, actively participating in their fundraising campaigns.

He also established "The Shaun White Foundation," which is focused on supporting community organizations that promote healthy lifestyles and assist children in need.

Furthermore, he's been an advocate for the Boys & Girls Club of America, helping provide opportunities and resources to young people across the country. His ongoing commitment to these causes reflects his desire to leave a positive impact beyond his sports career.

In many ways, Shaun White's life and career reflect his indomitable spirit. He once said, "I've always lived by the mantra, 'Do what you love, love what you do'. It's about pushing yourself, reaching for your dreams, and never forgetting who you are and where you came from."

In the world of extreme sports, Shaun White is more than just a legend. He is an inspiration, a role model, and an embodiment of resilience, passion, and dedication. His journey teaches us that with hard work and belief in oneself, even the highest peaks are within reach.

His legacy continues to inspire the next generation of athletes, proving that no matter the odds, we can fly.

WAYNE GRETZKY "THE GREAT ONE"

The icy winds howled around Madison Square Garden, creating a wild symphony of whistles and roars. It was April 18, 1999, and inside the arena, a crowd of thousands was buzzing with anticipation. Each pair of eyes was fixed on one person – Wayne Gretzky, number 99, "The Great One." The air was thick with a sense of both joy and sadness, because today was the day - the final game of Wayne's astonishing career.

At 38, Gretzky was about to hang up his skates, but there was still one last performance left to deliver. As he glided onto the ice, his heart pounded in his chest echoing the rhythm of his extraordinary journey. This journey was filled with record-breaking feats, dazzling plays, and unyielding determination.

He wore his helmet low, his gaze steely and focused. Every cell in his body buzzed with adrenaline as he prepared to make his final mark in the world of professional hockey. It was a bittersweet moment, a crossroads between the end of one chapter and the beginning of another.

Yet, his mind wasn't entirely focused on the present. As he made his way onto the rink, he felt a pull from the past. Images danced before his eyes - of a small backyard rink in Brantford, Ontario, of his first pair of skates, of his father cheering from the sidelines. They were like silent movies, reminding him of where it all started, where Wayne Gretzky, a small boy with big dreams, first stepped onto the ice and made it his own.

"Ready, Wayne?" The referee's voice brought him back to the present.

Gretzky nodded, took a deep breath, and tightened his grip on his stick. He was ready - ready to bid farewell, ready to show the world that although this was his last game, the spirit of "The Great One" would forever live on in the world of ice hockey.

Even as the tension grew, one question lingered in the hearts of everyone watching - How did a small boy from Brantford become "The Great One"? And so, our journey begins...

The story of Wayne Gretzky, like many great tales, starts in a small town. On a chilly January day in 1961, in the heart of Brantford, Ontario, Canada, a future legend was born. Walter and Phyllis Gretzky named their baby boy Wayne, unaware of the greatness he would one day achieve.

Wayne was just like any other kid in the neighborhood. He loved to play, laugh, and explore the world around him. But there was one thing that set young Wayne apart - his fascination with the chilly, sleek, gleaming ice.

At the tender age of two, a time when most toddlers are still getting used to walking on solid ground, Wayne put on his first pair of skates.

They were a pair of double-bladed galoshes, designed to give stability and balance to wobbly beginner's feet. But for Wayne, they were magical shoes that would carry him on an extraordinary journey.

His father, Walter, was the first to introduce Wayne to the sport. In the backyard of their modest home, Walter had built a makeshift ice rink. It was here that Wayne took his first steps on the ice, clambering onto the surface with a mixture of fear, excitement, and determination.

Each glide was unsteady, each fall hard, but Wayne was undeterred. He'd dust off the snow, get back on his feet, and give it another go. With each fall and each rise, Wayne was learning, growing, and falling in love with the game of hockey.

Under the watchful eyes of his father, he skated in loops, drew patterns on the ice with his blades, and laughed joyously at the magic of it all. For young Wayne, the rink was a world of wonder, and he was at the heart of it, blissfully skating into the future.

In these early years, Wayne wasn't just learning to skate. He was discovering a passion, a dream, something that would become as much a part of him as his own heartbeat.

As the chill of winter descended on Brantford in 1964, six-year-old Wayne Gretzky was stepping onto a real hockey rink for the first time. His dad, Walter, had signed him up for a local league, the Brantford Nadrofsky Steelers. He was the smallest kid on the team, standing head-and-shoulders below boys who were nearly twice his age. But Wayne wasn't deterred, his small size concealed a tenacious spirit and an immense love for the game.

Every game was a thrilling adventure for Wayne. The sound of the whistle, the cool gust of wind as he skated, the thrill of the chase – these were the things that filled his young heart with joy. But, as with any sport, there were challenges and Wayne, despite his incredible talent, wasn't immune to them.

The first few games were tough. Wayne was fast and clever, but he was small, and the bigger boys had the advantage. They pushed him around, blocked his shots, and outplayed him on the ice. But Wayne never lost heart. Each push, each blocked shot, was a lesson to be learned, a challenge to be overcome.

Then, one day in late 1965, it finally happened. The Steelers were playing against the Woodstock Warriors. Wayne, seven years old by then, seized the puck from an opponent almost twice his size. He slipped through the defenders, his small size suddenly becoming an advantage.

His skates flashed across the ice, his heart pounded in his chest, and with a swift and precise swing, he shot the puck. It flew across the ice, evading the goalie's outstretched arm and hit the net.

The crowd roared. Wayne had scored his first goal. His teammates swarmed around him, cheering and laughing, while his parents beamed with pride from the sidelines. It was a moment of sheer joy, a moment that marked the beginning of a legendary career.

Through the following years, Wayne honed his skills. The backyard rink remained his training ground, where under the tutelage of his father, he learned to read the ice, anticipate plays, and shoot with an accuracy that was beyond his years.

As he grew, so did his passion for the game. With each game, each practice, each goal, Wayne was carving a path that would lead him from the modest rinks of Brantford to the grand arenas of the NHL.

Walter Gretzky, the loving father and the tireless coach, was an indispensable force in Wayne's life. His guidance, mentorship, and the numerous life lessons he imparted made him Wayne's greatest ally on and off the ice.

Walter's approach to teaching his son the game was unconventional but incredibly effective. He knew that to excel in hockey, one had to think ahead, anticipate the game, and be where the puck was going to be, not where it was. This simple yet profound philosophy, "Skate to where the puck is going, not where it has been," became the guiding principle for Wayne. He learned to read the game, to understand the patterns and rhythms, and to predict his opponents' next move.

Countless hours were spent on their homemade rink, lovingly referred to as "Wally Coliseum," practicing this art of anticipation. Walter would dump a bucket of rubber balls onto the ice, and Wayne would have to chase them down, predicting where they would end up rather than where they were.

It wasn't always easy. Many winter afternoons turned into freezing evenings under the harsh Canadian weather. Tired, cold, and frustrated, young Wayne would sometimes feel like giving up. But Walter was there, not to coddle, but to encourage him, to push him harder. "You miss 100% of the shots you don't take," he'd say, urging Wayne to never shy away from trying, from risking, from playing the game with all his heart.

Their relationship wasn't just about hockey. His dad instilled in Wayne the importance of humility, respect, and kindness. He taught his son that one's character is as important as one's skill.

"A good hockey player plays where the puck is. A great hockey player plays where the puck is going to be," Walter would often tell him.

This was more than a game strategy; it was a life lesson in foresight, preparation, and humility.

Wayne's teenage years were filled with a mix of thrilling victories, growing recognition, and taxing challenges. As he graduated from the local league to play for the Sault Ste. Marie Greyhounds in the Ontario Hockey League, he was entering a whole new arena of competition. And although his skills were exceptional, he was about to face adversities that would test his resolve and shape his character.

In 1977, when Wayne, at 16, first stepped onto the ice wearing the Greyhound's jersey, he carried with him the weight of high expectations. His reputation as a hockey prodigy had made waves throughout Ontario, and the eyes of every fan, coach, and player were on him.

Yet, with every stride he took on the ice, every puck he deftly controlled, every goal he scored, he proved that he was not just a prodigy; he was a force to be reckoned with. In his very first season, he scored an astounding 70 goals, a record that left the entire league speechless. But his journey was not without its hurdles.

Despite his talent, Wayne faced harsh criticism and hostility from those who were unable to accept such a young player's success. He was often targeted by older, more physically aggressive players, knocked down, and jeered. But each bruise was a testament to his resilience, each taunt a test of his fortitude. Wayne didn't let the negativity affect him; instead, he responded where it mattered the most: on the ice. With grace and unwavering focus, he let his skill speak for him.

One such incident occurred during the 1978 season. An opponent, aiming to intimidate Wayne, delivered a particularly ruthless check, causing him to crash into the ice.

The crowd gasped, but Wayne, after a moment of silence, stood up. He dusted off the ice, straightened his jersey, and got back into the game. Later that game, it was Wayne's stunning goal that sealed the victory for the Greyhounds.

In the summer of 1979, Wayne, a mere 17-year-old, took a giant leap in his career by turning professional. With the Edmonton Oilers' jersey proudly worn over his shoulders, Wayne was about to make his mark in the National Hockey League (NHL), the apex of professional ice hockey.

Sharing the ice with legends like Guy Lafleur, Bryan Trottier, and Marcel Dionne, Wayne found himself competing against players who were not only nearly a decade his senior but also among the best in the league. The stage was bigger, the lights brighter, and the stakes higher than ever before. He was the youngest in the league, a fact that brought with it its own set of pressures and challenges.

Despite his phenomenal record in the Ontario Hockey League, stepping onto the professional stage was a different ball game altogether. The game was faster, the players stronger, and the critics harsher.

Many doubted whether the young prodigy could stand his ground amidst seasoned veterans. Every match was a challenge, a test of his mettle. He was knocked down, but he got back up, he missed shots, but he kept shooting, he lost games, but he never lost spirit.

Amid the struggles and growing pains, there were flashes of brilliance, glimpses of the extraordinary talent that had brought Wayne to this grand stage. His speed, precision, and game sense started gaining recognition. Even his harshest critics had to admit that there was something special about the young player wearing jersey number 99.

One of the most defining moments of his debut season came during a match against the Montreal Canadiens. In a move that would come to be known as vintage Gretzky, Wayne received the puck near his team's goal, swiftly navigated past the rival players with his exceptional skating and puck handling skills, and scored an improbable goal. The crowd erupted in cheers. It was a moment of pure exhilaration, a moment that announced to the world that a new star had arrived.

Despite the inevitable challenges of his rookie year, Wayne showed remarkable determination and resilience. He ended the season with a respectable 51 goals and an additional 86 assists, a record for a first-year player. He was awarded the Hart Trophy, becoming the youngest player ever to be named the league's most valuable player.

In the 1981-82 season, Wayne set a record that left the world in awe. He scored an astonishing 92 goals in a single season, shattering the previous record of 76. This achievement was a defining moment in his career. It was more than just a number; it was a testament to his skill, his determination, and his relentless pursuit of excellence.

But Wayne's journey to stardom wasn't just about the records he set or the matches he won; it was also about the rivals he faced and the adversities he overcame. One such challenge was his on-ice rivalry with Mark Messier of the New York Rangers.

Their games were intense, their competition fierce, and their encounters became legendary episodes in the annals of the NHL. Yet, amidst this intense pressure, Wayne remained focused, letting his performance on the ice answer his critics.

His unyielding determination and astounding skill were finally rewarded in 1984 when Wayne led the Edmonton Oilers to their first Stanley Cup win. The joy of lifting the Cup was a culmination of years of hard work, sacrifice, and undying passion for the game. It was a moment that Wayne would forever cherish.

Yet, Wayne did not rest on his laurels. He continued to train harder, perform better, and set higher goals. In the subsequent years, he would guide the Oilers to three more Stanley Cup victories, cementing his legacy as one of the greatest players the game has ever seen.

When the Edmonton Oilers' heart, Wayne Gretzky, was traded to the Los Angeles Kings, it sent shockwaves through the hockey world. The unexpected move, driven by Oilers' owner Peter Pocklington's financial desperation, felt out of place.

"You could have heard a pin drop in the locker room when they told us," Gretzky recalled. "I remember looking at my teammates, my brothers, and seeing the same shock in their eyes that I felt in my heart."

The Oilers' fans were devastated, their hearts shattered. They had lost their hero, their icon, their 'Great One'. To them, Pocklington's decision wasn't just a business move - it was a betrayal. Even to this day, the mere mention of his name evokes a bitter taste among the Oilers fans.

However, Gretzky viewed it as an opportunity for growth and an invitation to challenges.

Relocating to LA, a city where hockey was not the main sport, was akin to being a fish out of water for Gretzky. But his passion and dedication transcended boundaries, turning his debut game's eerily silent stands into roars of enthusiastic applause. Aided by his indomitable spirit and unparalleled skills, he not only played hockey but also popularized it in LA.

The journey was laden with victories and losses, but Gretzky's perseverance paid off, leading the Kings to the Stanley Cup finals in 1993. The final whistle of that match echoed LA's rise as a hockey city, and cemented Gretzky's legacy as 'The Great One' and 'The King'. The trade was not just a change of teams, it was the birth of a new era in Gretzky's illustrious career.

The final chapter of Wayne Gretzky's professional hockey journey commences with the announcement of his retirement. An era was coming to an end, but the weight of the moment did not diminish Gretzky's grace nor his gratitude for the years spent gliding across the rink.

The gravity of this decision didn't just stir the heart of 'The Great One'; it sent waves of mixed emotions across the globe. The news was met with a tidal wave of tributes, lauding Gretzky's skills, sportsmanship, and his contributions to the sport. Fans, teammates, rivals, they all tipped their caps to the hockey titan who had given the game so much.

Retirement for Gretzky was not an end, but the beginning of another phase of life. He reminisced about his journey, the triumphs, the struggles, the countless hours on the ice. Each memory, a testament to his love for the game, each victory, a page in the history of hockey he had helped write. "I've been fortunate to do what I love for many years," Gretzky confessed in his retirement speech, "and while it's hard to say goodbye, it's the right time."

As the curtain fell on his illustrious career, Gretzky returned to the ice one last time. It was a moment that paralleled the tension and drama of his last professional game, bringing the narrative full circle. As he skated around the rink, waving to the roaring crowd, it was clear - this was not a mere farewell. It was a thank you, a final lap to celebrate the joy and passion the sport had brought him, and an acknowledgement of the indelible legacy he had created.

The last echoes of the whistle are all that remain to his final appearance on the ice, a touching reminder of the end of an era.

Yet, the legend of Wayne Gretzky, 'The Great One', lives on.

CONCLUSION

Whew! What an incredible ride, huh? We zoomed alongside race cars with Lewis Hamilton, twirled on the gymnastics mat with Simone Biles, dodged punches with Muhammad Ali, and even caught monstrous waves with Bethany Hamilton. Not to mention, we played a thrilling game of catch-up with Usain Bolt. Talk about fast!

Each one of these super-cool sports stars started just like you, as a kid with big dreams. Sure, they stumbled, they tripped, they even face-planted, but guess what? They dusted off their knees, bandaged their scrapes, tied their shoelaces, and got back up stronger each time.

They weren't born champions. Nope. They became champions by facing tough times with a grin, working hard when no one was watching, and never letting go of their dreams, even when the going got tough, super tough.

They showed us that being a champion isn't just about scoring the winning goal or standing on the tallest podium. Nope, it's about being brave when you're scared, trying again when you fail, standing tall when life tries to knock you down. It's about finding the super-hero inside you and letting it shine!

So, as you close this book and set it on your shelf, remember, you've got a bit of Ronaldo's dedication, Serena's strength, Jordan's persistence, and Bethany's courage now.

Take these lessons with you wherever you go. Whether it's nailing that tricky math problem, standing up to that big, mean bully, or shooting for the stars with your own crazy, awesome dreams.

And remember, the bumps and stumbles are all part of the fun ride.

Thanks for joining us on this wild adventure. Keep laughing, keep dreaming, and most importantly, keep being the incredible, unique YOU.

Remember, you are not just reading stories of great people, you're about to start your own story of greatness!